School, family, community:
Mapping school inclusion in the UK

Alan Dyson and Elaine Robson

YOUTH • WORK • PRESS

JR
JOSEPH
ROWNTREE
FOUNDATION

First published in Great Britain in 1999 by Youth Work Press, the publishing imprint of the National Youth Agency.
17–23 Albion Street, Leicester LE1 6GD.
Tel: 0116.285.3700. Fax: 0116.285.3777.
E-mail: nya@nya.org.uk Website: http://www.nya.org.uk

Published for the Joseph Rowntree Foundation by Youth Work Press

ISBN 0 86155 213 X

Price: £13.95

The Joseph Rowntree Foundation has supported this project as part of its programme of research and innovative development projects, which it hopes will be of value to policy-makers, practitioners and service users. The facts presented and views expressed in this report, however, are those of the authors and not necessarily those of the Foundation.

Cover design: Sanjay Kukadia

Printed by Joseph Ball, Leicester

Contents

Acknowledgments

This review is very much a collective effort. The authors would, in particular, like to express their gratitude to the team of reviewers:

Anne Baynes	**Jill Birch**
Martin Brown	**Sarah Cochrane**
Ben Davis	**Stephen Dyson**
John Elliott	**Neil Farmer**
Frances Gallanaugh	**Ian Hall**

The review benefited greatly from the comments and suggestions of a group of practitioners and researchers who participated in an expert seminar or corresponded with the research team. They were:

Joan Baxter, The Place to Be, London

Prof. Miriam David, London Institute of Education

Jane Gledhill, Bradford LEA

Georgina Glennie, School of Education, Oxford Brookes University

Phil Green, DIECEC Coordinator, Bradford

Stuart Gregory, North Yorkshire County Council

Nick Hudson, Blackburn with Darwen Borough Council

Dick Jenkinson, CEDC, Coventry

Eithne Leming, Suffolk LEA

Charlie Lloyd, Joseph Rowntree Foundation, York

Dr. Alastair Macbeth, University of Glasgow

Tom Macdonald, Education and Industry Department, Scottish Office

Tony Martin, Analytical Services, DfEE

Carol McAlpine, Firfield Community School, Newcastle upon Tyne

Alwyn Morgan, Alwyn Morgan and Associates

Sandra Morton, City and County of Swansea

Prof. Pamela Munn, Murray House Institute of Education

Susan Taylor, Joseph Rowntree Foundation, York

Dr. Keith Topping, University of Dundee

Dr. Carol Vincent, London Institute of Education

Dr. Graham Vulliamy, Department of Education Studies, University of York

Helen Walters, Read On, Write Away, Matlock

Dr. Rosemary Webb, Department of Education Studies, University of York

Derek Wise, Education and Libraries Directorate, Newcastle upon Tyne City Council

Prof. Sheila Wolfendale, Department of Psychology, University of East London

Finally, the authors would like to acknowledge the support and encouragement of Pat Kneen of the Joseph Rowntree Foundation.

The responsibility for any errors or shortcomings, of course, remains firmly with the authors themselves.

Executive summary

Mog Ball's 1998 report, *School Inclusion*, reviewed the state of practice in the UK on the development of links between schools, families and communities. Although her work provides us with an excellent snapshot of developments on the ground, it makes no attempt to review the literature. In particular, it is not concerned with sifting the evidence as to what is effective in this field and what are the wider effects of school-family-community links. The current report is an attempt to fill this gap.

Our report is the outcome of a review of the evaluative and research literature in this field from the UK, concentrating on the post-1988 period. It includes both the scholarly literature and, where we were able to access it, the 'grey' literature of evaluation reports and unpublished papers. Of the many items accessed, over 300 were finally deemed sufficiently significant to be included in the review.

Although there is a good deal from which policy-makers and practitioners can learn, the UK literature is also characterised by significant limitations – unevenness in the coverage of different types of links, a reliance on local evaluations of small-scale projects and an absence of wide-ranging programmatic evaluations. The literature also has little to say about the relative cost-effectiveness or cost-benefits of various approaches. These limitations may be related to the fact that school-family-community links tend to be 'bolted on' to schools' main concerns and resourced through short-term, locally-determined projects, with minimal intervention from central government.

The literature on **parental involvement in learning** is the most substantial and sophisticated in this field, though it focuses heavily on literacy (and, to a lesser extent, numeracy) in the primary years. It offers evidence that involving parents in their children's learning is likely to enhance the attainments of children, to improve their attitudes to learning and to be welcomed by many parents.

On the other hand, the literature tells us little about 'failures' in this field. Not all schemes are equally successful for all parents and children – but we do not fully understand why. Similarly, we know very little about the schools, teachers and, in particular, parents who drop out of schemes or do not participate in the first instance. There are also ethical and political issues around this area. The model of parent-child relations and of family values embedded in the parental involvement movement may well operate as a form of 'cultural imperialism', devaluing the practices and values of families who may already be somewhat marginalised. The net effect may simply be to alienate those families and disadvantage their children further.

The literature on other forms of **partnership with parents** suggests that they produce positive effects, not least in that they are appreciated and valued by parents. There is particular evidence from the field of special needs education, where relationships have been placed on a more formal and statutory footing, that such formalisation is effective in requiring the education service to engage fully with parents.

However, there is evidence that the development . of partnerships imposes strains on schools which have to manage such partnerships alongside their other priorities. More fundamentally, the literature demonstrates an underlying power imbalance between education professionals and parents. Partnership takes place very much on terms dictated by the former, with the consequent marginalisation of the latter – an issue which may be particularly important where parents belong to social groups that already experience marginalisation. There is little indication in the literature of how this issue might be addressed, though there is some limited evidence of parental groups' operating successfully outside the direct control of education professionals.

There is well-founded evidence that **collaboration between community agencies** presents both possibilities and pitfalls arising from the professional misunderstandings and mistrust which characterise this area. However, there is evidence that non-educationalists can make an effective contribution to activities which lie at the 'periphery' of schools' work. In particular, they can contribute to work with vulnerable children, where they can mediate between schools and the child's family and community, and to the 'non-academic' aspects of curriculum. There is also evidence that mentoring is effective in changing pupils' attitudes and raising their attainment. It may be that non-teachers bring with them a 'credibility' arising from their experiences outside of school to which teachers themselves cannot aspire.

The situation with regard to **community education** and the participation of parents and community in **school management and decision-making** is less positive. The education reforms of the late 1980s and early 1990s appear to have privileged individual parents acting as consumers over the community interest and have further marginalised those parents who, for whatever reason, are not able to exercise their consumer role effectively. As a result, there are doubts as to whether community education meets the real needs of communities and whether communities are able to exert a real influence over the schools which serve them. On the other hand, there is some evidence that, in areas experiencing multiple disadvantage, there is potential for schools to become involved in multi-strand initiatives aimed at addressing the sources of disadvantage in a coherent way.

Since the current research literature is dominated by reports of small-scale, local studies, there is a need for **further research** in this field which is more substantial in terms of its scale, scope and depth. Different sorts of studies are needed (for example, large-scale quasi-experiments, in-depth case-studies and multi-level studies), but they need to be related to each other in a way which is programmatic and which may call for coherent funding from the major research sponsors.

There is a need for research which adopts a community rather than a professional perspective, focusing on the perceptions of community members and the impacts of links on the community (rather than simply on the school). Specific gaps in our knowledge need to be filled in terms of studies of families, teachers and schools who do not participate in links. Moreover, there is a need for the critical and evaluative research traditions in this field to be brought closer together so that they can inform each other more fully.

In terms of **policy and practice**, at local level the further development of school-family-community links seems like a good investment for schools and LEAs to make. However, given the constraints under which schools operate, these links will need leadership and resources from beyond the school. Given the uncertainty of particular approaches working in every situation, they will also need careful local monitoring.

At national level, there is a role for central government in helping to formalise and disseminate what has been learned in this field so that local initiatives do not have to reinvent the wheel. There is also a need for central government to prioritise and resource this area of schools' work appropriately in order to avoid the current patchwork of bolt-on provision. In particular, central government could usefully promote large-scale, evidence-based projects with in-built evaluation.

More generally, there is a tension in government policy between the 'crusade for standards', which requires schools to focus on their 'core business' of curriculum delivery, and a broader social exclusion agenda which implies a more extended community role for schools. Although there are points of congruence between these agendas, they also create significant tensions in schools. There is a need for central government to think through the role that it envisages for schools and to consider how links with broader social policy are to be managed in the light of that role.

1 Introduction

For as long as there have been mass education systems in the UK, it has been evident that schools cannot entirely be divorced from their social context. The interaction between school and environment has been understood in a range of ways over the past hundred years and more, but at least three main tendencies can be traced:

- **Education cannot compensate for society.**
  Basil Bernstein's famous dictum (Bernstein, 1970) encapsulates the view that schools have to be seen as part of the wider social structures in which they are embedded. Schools cannot overcome the effects of the family, community and, particularly, social class backgrounds of their pupils, but merely reflect and reproduce the advantages and disadvantages enjoyed by different social groups (Douglas, 1964; Floud, 1961; Floud, Halsey and Martin, 1956).

- **Education as an escape route.** An alternative view has accepted the potentially disadvantageous effects of certain social backgrounds, but has argued that schools can offer an escape route for some individuals. What children can achieve in school is not entirely determined by their background, but by their innate abilities and the quality of teaching they receive. This view informed, though in somewhat different ways, both the grammar school movement and the comprehensive school movement (Bellaby, 1977; Husen, 1979). More recently, it can be seen as underpinning at least the early forms of the school effectiveness movement (Mortimore, 1988; Rutter, 1979) and current government initiatives to drive up 'standards' in inner-city schools (DfEE, 1999).

- **Education as a family and community resource.** Sitting somewhere between these views is a tradition which sees the relationship between schools and their social contexts as more interactive and more evenly balanced than the other two positions. Stretching from the prewar Cambridgeshire Village College movement, through the compensatory education and community school movements of the 1960s and 1970s (Halsey, 1972; Tomlinson, 1991) through to the 'new' community schools of the 1990s (Scottish Office, 1998) there is a view that schools can serve, not merely to remove 'able' children from their communities, but to make a positive contribution to those communities. Moreover, communities in general and families in particular are seen, not as a source of disadvantage, but as capable of making a positive contribution to schools and the children within them. In this way, the school acts as a resource for the community and the community, in turn, acts as a resource for the school.

It is this 'third way' with which, in general terms, this review is concerned. In her recent *School Inclusion* report for the Joseph Rowntree Foundation, Mog Ball (1998) set out to describe the range of links currently in place between schools, families and communities in the UK. One of the outcomes of her report was a typology which defined the field in terms of seven types of linkage:

- the participation of parents and other community members in decision-making and management of the school;
- communication between home and school;
- school support for families;
- family and community help for schools;
- the encouragement of learning activities at home;

- collaborations and exchanges with community agencies beyond the school which provide support services to children; and
- community education.

While Ball is able to map a wide range of collaborative activities within and beyond schools and to indicate the potential benefits of these activities, she is less sanguine when she reviews the research evidence underpinning school-family-community links:

> Many come with evaluation reports based on the experience of schools and communities in the UK where they were first implemented. These have been carried out by people of integrity and experience. But there are no comparative studies and there is little evidence about long-term impact. Not surprising, since hardly any of the programmes have been operational for more than ten years and there has been little follow-up research.

> Where systematic review of programmes has occurred, the results are often disappointing ... Most local programmes have unclear goals and make little scientifically acceptable effort to assess outcomes. These criticisms could be levelled more widely – at the evaluation reports distributed as part of the marketing of 'packages' to schools, for example. (Ball, 1998: 55)

It is out of these comments that the present review arises. There is currently a new upsurge of interest at national policy level in the role that schools might play in addressing the patterns of endemic disadvantage which characterise some communities and to which many individuals within and beyond those communities are subject (Social Exclusion Unit, 1998). This upsurge is based on the assumption both that the contribution that schools can make is significant and that we know what sorts of activities are likely to be most effective in addressing the problems of children and young people, their families and communities. It is more important than ever, therefore, that we try to sift from the mass of anecdotal evidence, enthusiastic participant reports and unsound local evaluations, the evidence of effectiveness that is capable of standing up to critical scrutiny. That is the purpose of this review.

The nature of the review

This review aims to identify good evaluative evidence on the effectiveness of school-family-community links in the UK. A parallel international review has been undertaken by Peter Moss and Pat Petrie at the Thomas Coram Institute, University of London.

The working definition of school-family-community links which we have adopted is broadly that set out in Mog Ball's typology, though we have extended that definition where the literature has taken us into important related areas. There are, for instance, important literatures relating to parental involvement in special needs education and the involvement of parents and communities as 'consumers' in the education market-place. Similarly, there are, as we shall see, some categories in Ball's typology where the literature is somewhat thin and where we shall have little to say.

The definition of 'effectiveness' can be problematic. For some forms of school-family-community link, it is fairly easy to see what counts as effective. If, for instance, parents are involved in supporting the literacy development of their children, then it is reasonable to expect that effective programmes will bring about a rise in literacy attainments. However, in other categories, the notion of effectiveness is less straightforward. What, for instance, counts as the 'effective' involvement of families and communities in the governance of schools and how might one assess the 'effectiveness' of school support for families? Our position in these cases has been to work with the broader notion of 'effects' rather than the narrower notion of 'effectiveness'. In other words, we have tried to find evidence that school-family-community links change **something**, for better or worse, rather than searching in every case for unequivocal evidence of improvements in a specific area such as children's attainments.

A further issue has been to find a way of delimiting our searches. The field as defined by Mog Ball is already huge, comprising some categories which have their own substantial specialist literatures – and it would have been easy to add even more new categories. The strategy we adopted, however, was to stay within the confines of Ball's typology unless there were compelling reasons for going beyond it and, moreover, to draw a notional boundary marked by the 1988 Education Reform Act. Although we have included a few items of literature from before this date, our systematic searches ended with the major changes that were introduced at that point. A further, more pragmatic, limit to our searches was the fact that this was a small-scale and time-limited (four-month) project.

In terms of search methodology, we attempted to identify both the standard research literature, available in scholarly books and articles and in nationally-published reports, and the so-called 'grey' literature of unpublished papers and internal reports by local bodies such as LEAs, TECs and charitable organisations.[1] We contacted a range of local and national bodies in order to identify any reports and other literature they may have produced. Moreover, we conducted particularly intensive searches in geographical areas where there were good reasons to suppose that particularly interesting work had been done in school-family-community links.

The literature we identified was sifted, and at both the search and the analysis stages, we screened out any literature that was not clearly evaluative or research-based. We then rated each item in terms of the apparent strength of the evidence it contained. Finally, we presented our emerging findings to an expert seminar comprising senior practitioners and researchers in relevant fields. Their comments enabled us both to identify gaps in our searches and to test our tentative conclusions against their deeper knowledge of particular aspects of the school-family-community field.

Given the constraints of time and resources under which we were operating, there is no doubt that there will be gaps in our identification of relevant literature. There may even be some systematic biases; grey literature, for instance, is a good deal harder to access than formal research literature, with the result that funded research may be over-represented in our review at the expense of small-scale local evaluations. What follows, therefore, should be regarded as an indicative

---

1 Further details of the search methodology are presented in an appendix.

rather than comprehensive review of the literature. Nonetheless, we have considerable confidence that we have identified a sufficient range of recent literature and have tested our findings sufficiently well to make it possible for us to identify the salient themes emerging from research and evaluation.

In terms of presenting the findings, we have opted to use Ball's typology as a framework, though with some reorganisation. This has the advantage of making cross-referencing between Ball's work and our own more straightforward. However, it has the inevitable disadvantage of forcing some of the literature into categories which are only partially appropriate and, particularly, of concealing the extent to which, on the ground, different types of school-family-community link are found together and interact with each other. We have stressed these interactions wherever appropriate and trust that readers of this report will be tolerant of the limitations of a categorical

approach to such a complex field.

Accordingly, chapter 2 presents an overview of the principal features of the evidence-base as it emerges from the literature. Chapter 3 reviews the substantial literature on parental involvement in children's learning (Ball's 'encouragement of learning activities at home'). Chapter 4 is concerned with Ball's categories of communication between home and school, school support for families and family and community help for schools – which we have assembled under the generic heading of 'parents as partners'. In chapter 5, we review the broader community role of schools, dealing with Ball's categories of collaborations and exchanges with community agencies, community education and decision-making and management of the school. Finally, in chapter 6, we summarise our findings and consider their implications for research, policy and practice in this field.

2 The features of the evidence-base

Quantitative analyses

In total, and after discarding purely descriptive literature, we identified over 300 items which contained evaluation and research evidence relating to school-family-community links. The distribution of these items across Mog Ball's typology is shown in Table 1 and their distribution across the age ranges of pupils (using the English key stage system for convenience) is shown in Table 2.

It is, of course, important not to read too much into these figures, which reflect the literature accessed rather than the literature produced – much

less the range of activity on the ground. Nonetheless, they do seem to indicate that there is research and evaluation evidence available across the full range of school-family-community links. The emphasis on primary schooling evident in Table 2 is, perhaps, not surprising. However, that emphasis is not as marked as might have been supposed. Similarly, there are clear differences in the distribution of available evidence across the categories of links in the typology. One might have expected there to be more research around the encouragement of learning activities at home than school support for families, for instance. However,

Table 1 – Distribution of items of literature across categories of school-family-community link

Category of link	Percentage of items
Decision-making and management of the school	21
Communication between home and school	43
School support for families	19
Family and community help for schools	19
Encouragement of learning activities at home	33
Collaborations and exchanges with community agencies	32
Community education	22

Table 2 – Target age of links programme

Age group	Percentage of items
Pre-school	27
5 –7 (Key stage 1)	55
7 – 11 (Key stage 2)	54
11 – 14 (Key stage 3)	46
14 – 16 (Key stage 4)	45
Post-16	31

there is nonetheless a substantial quantity of literature even in the less-researched categories.

A further analysis is presented in Table 3 which shows our categorisation of items of literature in terms of the effects of school-family-community links for which they were able to present evidence.

Again, some caution needs to be exercised in interpreting these figures. Nonetheless, there are some interesting contrasts. Significantly more of the literature, for instance, offers evidence of parental involvement in learning than of the **impact** of such involvement on attainments. Similarly, there is a

Table 3 – Evidence of effects of school-family-community links

Type of effect	Percentage of items providing evidence of effect
Pupil learning/attainment	38
Pupil behaviour	25
Parental involvement in children's learning	58
Parental involvement in wider school issues	28
Development of parenting skills	22
Meeting families' needs	12
School performance	9
Attitudes and practices within the school	30
School's relationship with the community	25
Community involvement in the school	21
Community learning	19
Other community/regeneration issues	14
Sustained links between school-family-community	26

greater emphasis on parental involvement in learning than on other issues which might be considered less close to schools' immediate priorities – parental involvement in wider school issues, for instance, or links which are directed towards meeting families' needs, or wider community-related concerns. It is also notable, given the emphasis on school effectiveness in both research and policy terms over recent years, that there is very little literature which offers direct evidence of the impact of family and community links on overall school performance.

Other analyses support some emerging impressions of the literature as a whole. Over 50 per cent of items, for instance, are concerned with links between schools and parents, compared with 17 per cent concerned with the wider community, 12 per cent with charitable bodies, 11 per cent with business and industry and single figure percentages

with the health service, social services departments, the police and other groups. The largest groupings among the links that are researched or evaluated are either school-led (16 per cent) or locally-led (35 per cent) and are resourced from local (LEA or school) education budgets. Not surprisingly, therefore, the largest group of items (some 42 per cent) that we reviewed comprises evaluations of local programmes. Only 22 per cent of items were concerned with national initiatives – and frequently these national initiatives seem to have been subject to considerable local interpretation.

Finally, we rated each item according to its significance in contributing to an evidence base for school-family-community links. After the purely descriptive literature had been discarded, some 5 per cent of items were rated as 'essential', 21 per cent as 'very important', 55 per cent as 'quite important' and 17 per cent as 'not important'.

Qualitative analyses

These quantitative analyses serve to support some impressions which emerge from reading the literature:

- **Much of the literature is concerned with small-scale local initiatives which yield limited evaluative evidence.** As the analysis above indicates, many links are – quite understandably – led by schools, LEAs or other local bodies and are funded from local budgets. The attempt to evaluate and report these is, in itself, commendable, but the sort of evidence which results is of strictly limited use beyond the local context. It is extremely difficult in these local initiatives, for instance, to identify matched groups of non-participants to act as controls, or to compare different sorts of initiatives rigorously, or to resource longitudinal evaluations with long-term follow-ups. Not surprisingly, therefore, many initiatives, which may be excellent in themselves, tend to rely on somewhat anecdotal evidence based, perhaps, on comments from participants backed up by limited quantitative data on attendance rates or attainments (see, for instance Bridge, 1998; DfEE, 1998; Leming, 1997; City and County of Swansea Community Outdoor Education Service, 1996, 1997, 1998). While such reports are of considerable local significance, they can be no more than indicative in a national context.

- **Some initiatives which appear to be national are simply aggregations of local initiatives.** A number of national bodies have sponsored programmes where either considerable discretion is left to local providers as to how the programme

shall be implemented, or, indeed, where the apparently national programme is simply an assembly of local initiatives in order to illustrate a notion of 'best practice'. The consequence is that whole-programme evaluations have to rely on locally-collected and, consequently, diverse and non-comparable data. The comments of the national evaluators of family literacy schemes sponsored by the Basic Skills Agency capture some of the tensions between the priorities of local providers and the requirements of a rigorous programme evaluation:

> For sound educational reasons, pre and post programme testing of parents' levels of literacy and other communication skills was rarely conducted. It was important that measures, or indices of progress, were locally chosen and consistent with the practices of agencies and schools within the small grants scheme. Most family literacy tutors preferred informal means of assessing adults, which were usually developed from previous work.
> (Poulson *et al.*, 1997: 19)

While one understands the 'sound educational reasons' referred to here, the lack of comparable data necessarily limits both the claims that can be made for the programme as a whole and the potential for comparing the effectiveness of one approach against that of another.

- **Some of the literature is concerned with national or large-scale programmes that have been subject to significantly limited evaluations.** Two examples serve to illustrate this point. The IMPACT project is (as we shall see) one of the major programmes aimed at enhancing parents' involvement in their children's learning (Merttens, 1996; Merttens and Vass, 1993). It is supported by an impressive research programme which has generated some of the most creative thinking in this field (Merttens, Mayers, Brown and Vass, 1993). However, it has, so far as we can determine, never been subject to a rigorous, programme-wide evaluation, relying instead on smaller-scale evaluations of local examples. Similarly, the government-sponsored summer literacy schools have relied partly on local evaluations (with all the problems identified above) and partly on extremely short-term and tightly focused national evaluations (Education Extra, 1997b, c; Sainsbury et al., 1998). While there is nothing wrong with these evaluations per se, their narrow focus limits significantly what can be claimed for or learned about the scheme. Both the IMPACT and summer literacy school evaluation styles point to an apparent absence in the UK literature of rigorous, whole-programme evaluations which might make it possible to claim with some confidence that some forms of school-family-community links produce clearly-defined and substantiated benefits. Breathless accounts of 'extraordinary enthusiasm' and 'most imaginative practice' (Education Extra, 1997c: 7) are all very well, but they offer a flimsy basis for large-scale changes in practice.

- **Comparative studies and cost-benefit analyses are notably absent from the literature.** Perhaps not surprisingly, given what we have said, the majority of studies which address the question of effectiveness tend to focus on single projects or programmes. Although there are, of course, reviews of the literature such as the present one, it is difficult for such reviews to undertake direct comparisons of the vast diversity of small-scale projects that have flourished (and often died) in order to determine the relative effectiveness of different approaches. Moreover, the notion of 'cost' is almost entirely absent from the literature, so that the identification of the relative costs and benefits of different approaches is virtually impossible. In principle, the reliance of many projects on external funding ought to promote a concern with value for money.

- **The relationship between evaluators and sponsors is ambiguous in many evaluations.** Because many school-family-community links arise out of specially-funded initiatives, there is a tendency for the funders of the initiative also to be the funders of the evaluation. Hence, training and enterprise councils, local education authorities, Single Regeneration Budget partnerships, schools and, indeed, national government routinely promote, fund and commission the evaluation of their own initiatives. From the point of view of these funders, of course, this is entirely right and proper, since the evaluation tells them whether they or their clients have spent their money wisely and enables them to shape their future policies on the basis of good information. However, it does raise questions about the freedom which the evaluation has to examine difficulties in particular projects and, more particularly, to explore flaws in the fundamental assumptions on which those projects have been promoted and funded. It is not so much that evaluators might be routinely massaging the truth as that the issues which matter to their sponsors might be different from the issues which would need to be explored in the interests of developing a robust national evidence base on school-family-community links.

• **Much of the literature is concerned with forms of school-family-community link that are not susceptible to effectiveness-oriented evaluations.** In the first chapter, we made a careful distinction between the 'effectiveness' of school-family-community links and their 'effects'. While it is legitimate to expect that programmes aimed at, say, raising children's attainments through parental involvement might engage in a rigorous evaluation of their effectiveness, other forms of link have, quite properly, somewhat broader aims which demand a different style of evaluation. The development of a parents' centre (Gale, 1996; Philips, 1989), for instance, or direct action taken by parents in their local school (Carspecken, 1991), or the development of parent-centred organisations (Vincent and Warren, 1997) all have effects, but it would be inappropriate to evaluate them in terms of one or two dimensions of effectiveness. While, therefore, the literature on such cases has significant implications for policy and practice, those implications do not emerge in the form of neatly-packaged prescriptions for action.

• **Some of the literature is theoretical or critical in orientation.** A good deal of the literature we reviewed was either not concerned with particular programmes or was using those programmes to illustrate broader issues. The orientation of this literature was largely theoretical and frequently critical in that it sought to deconstruct school-family-community links in terms of their underlying assumptions and power relations (see, for instance, Jeffs, 1992; Reay,

1996; Vincent, 1996a, 1996b; Walker, 1998a, 1998b). Again, this literature has significant implications for policy and practice – but implications which take the form of fundamental challenges to current assumptions and practices rather than straightforward prescriptions.

Summary

There is, as we shall see in succeeding chapters, a good deal in the UK literature on school-family-community links from which policy-makers and practitioners can learn. However, the literature is also characterised by significant limitations – unevenness in the coverage of different types of links, a reliance on local evaluations of small-scale projects and an absence of wide-ranging programmatic evaluations. It is difficult not to conclude that these limitations are related, in part at least, to the ways in which school-family-community links are managed and resourced in the UK. Rather than being at the core of the work of the school and therefore of national policy, such links tend to be 'bolted on' to the school's main concerns and resourced through short-term, locally-determined projects. For the most part, national government is content to leave the development of such links to schools, LEAs and other local bodies – though when it does become directly involved, it is unlikely to be interested in wide-ranging evaluations which might problematise its current policies.

Policy-makers and practitioners who wish to learn from the literature, therefore, have to engage in a demanding process of critical analysis and synthesis. They have to read a good deal, understand the limitations of much of what they are reading, recontextualise it for their own situations and relate it to a somewhat different body of theoretical and critical literature. There is, in other words, an evidence-base on school-family-community links, but it is one which is far from clear or accessible.

3 Parental involvement in children's learning

It is appropriate to begin our detailed review in the area of parental involvement in children's learning since it is this form of school-family link which has generated the closest thing we have to a substantial and trustworthy evidence base. Despite the preponderance of local initiatives, here as elsewhere, a relatively coherent body of literature has been produced by high-quality researchers building systematically on each other's work. Moreover, this is a form of school-family link which has relatively clear and measurable aims (notably, the enhancement of children's attainments) and where effectiveness-oriented evaluations are possible and common.

The rationale for parental involvement in children's learning seems to arise from a number of sources. The evidence, cited in Chapter 1, for the failure of schools to compensate for social disadvantage suggests, for instance, that there are mechanisms operating in home and community to 'transmit' that disadvantage from generation to generation. Indeed, a good deal of effort was expended by sociologists in the 1960s and 1970s in trying to identify those mechanisms in terms of limited language use or transmission of limited 'cultural capital'. This picture is reinforced by more specific evidence that children's attainments (and, particularly, low attainments) are closely related to those of their parents (ALBSU, 1993). Moreover, there is evidence that, where certain parenting practices (such as hearing children read) are present, they have a positive impact on children's attainments (Hewison and Tizard, 1980).

In the light of this evidence, it is not surprising that there has been considerable interest in exploring ways of enabling parents to play a greater and more positive part in their children's learning. The emphasis tends to have been in three areas:

encouraging the involvement of parents *per se*; helping parents to adopt specific practices which are seen to be supportive of learning; and enhancing the educational attainments of parents themselves in the expectation that this will enable them to contribute more effectively to their children's development.

Parental involvement in literacy

The bulk of parental involvement work, as evidenced in the literature, has focused on literacy development. From the pioneering Haringey study (Tizard, Schofield, and Hewison, 1982; Hewison, 1988) onwards, there has been growing evidence that promoting and structuring parental involvement can have positive effects on children's reading (see, for instance, Cairney, 1996; Hannon, 1992; Phillips, 1996; Topping, 1991, 1996b; Topping and Wolfendale, 1995; Wolfendale, 1996). In particular, most studies report at least some gains in children's attainments and almost all studies report positive attitudes on the part of parents, children and teachers.

Within this broadly optimistic picture, however, there are some complexities:

- The detailed methodologies used by different schemes are often significantly different from each other. Parental involvement in reading can mean simply sending books home and encouraging parents and children to share them, or generating joint literacy activities in which parents and children engage collaboratively, or training parents in specific techniques for working with their children – techniques which themselves vary from project to project. There is something of a consensus that parental involvement schemes need to be well-organised, but beyond this it is difficult to compare across schemes to identify methods which unequivocally work better than others.

- Although parental involvement produces positive outcomes in general terms, there is considerable variability both between and within schemes as to the gains for different participating groups. It seems that we know too little about the processes at work within different schemes – and, particularly, within different families – to be able to predict with any confidence that a particular form of involvement will benefit a particular child in a particular school (Greenhough and Hughes, 1998; Jones and Rowley, 1990; Poulson, Bennett, and Macleod, 1996). Cuckle (1996) is able to offer some suggestions as to some of the factors which make parents willing and effective supporters of their children's learning. However, the majority of studies in this field report quasi-experiments and focus on outcomes rather than a detailed analysis of processes. Similarly, although most schemes seem to generate positive attitudes amongst their participants, we know too little about how those attitudes are translated into gains in attainment to be able to guarantee that the latter will occur (Sandler, 1989; Wolfendale, 1998).

- There are particular issues surrounding the evaluation of family literacy schemes (Topping, 1996). Whereas some parental involvement schemes focus on raising children's attainments, family literacy and allied schemes see the attainments of children as inextricably bound up with the attainments and attitudes of those family members who might be expected to support their learning in the home. Consequently, they set

themselves ambitious aims of affecting the latter as well as the former. Although, therefore, the general rule that well-organised and carefully focused schemes tend to be effective holds good here as elsewhere (Brooks, 1996), diverse, ambitious and sometimes imprecise aims, with improvements in children's attainments as only an indirect outcome, make it difficult to find hard evidence of effectiveness in some other schemes.

There are three broader issues which are raised by parental involvement programmes in literacy – but which apply more generally to all forms of parental involvement in learning. The first is to do with the relationship between the culture of the home and community on the one hand and the culture of the school on the other. Parental involvement is premised on the notion that literacy, as defined by the school, is a 'good', that parents should support their children's literacy development and, frequently, that there are particular forms of support which families should offer. Not surprisingly, therefore, some commentators see parental involvement schemes as a form of 'cultural imperialism', operating with a deficit model of the family and marginalising the parenting and literacy practices of families and the wider social groups of which they are part (Barton, 1995; Lareau, 1997; Tett and Crowther, 1998). Not surprisingly, also, some parents feel threatened by the invitation to become involved in literacy rather than empowered by it (Stoker, 1996).

This, in turn, links to a second issue. The broadly positive tone of the literature is not unrelated to the fact that it focuses on 'successes' rather than 'failures'. By and large, it is concerned to demonstrate the ways in which parental involvement can make a positive difference to children's attitudes and attainments. In addition to the natural bias which tends to be built into any scientific literature to report only those instances where there are positive outcomes, therefore, there is an additional tendency to focus on those parents, teachers and schools who participate fully. The parents who 'drop out' or who decline to participate, the teachers who do not become involved in their school's scheme and the schools which do not develop schemes are largely absent from the literature. Some critics would add that the literature is similarly poor at investigating differences between those children, classes and families for whom participation is effective and those for whom it is not (Macleod, 1996).

This does not, of course, invalidate the findings from those who do participate and who are 'successful', but it does mean that we know little about non-participants, or about what might be needed to persuade them to become involved, or about why some children and families appear not to benefit. On the other hand, it is perhaps worth adding that there is some limited evidence that a careful targeting of non-participating families can be effective in increasing participation rates (Calderdale and Kirkless TEC, 1998).

Again, this links to the third issue. There is some evidence (albeit not from the UK) that parental involvement schemes might actually increase educational inequality (Toomey, 1993). The argument here is a fairly simple one: if parental involvement enhances children's attainments, then the non-participation of some parents must disadvantage their children; if, moreover, non-participation is associated with other forms of disadvantage, then those children might find themselves in the double jeopardy of being disadvantaged in a way which prevents their

families from accessing the very programmes that are designed to overcome those disadvantages. Although it is far too simplistic to say that non-participation is a function of low socio-economic status (Hannon, 1992; West, Noden, and Edge, 1998), it does seem likely that some combinations of family characteristics – class, poverty, alienation from the education system, additional-language use, lack of parental education – might not only disadvantage children in their day-to-day schooling, but might also militate against the participation of parents in structured parental involvement schemes (see, for instance, Bryans, 1989; Tomlinson, 1993).

Parental involvement in numeracy

The evidence on parental involvement in numeracy is somewhat slighter than in the field of literacy, but is not significantly different in kind (see, for instance, Luton Education Department, 1998; Merttens, 1993, 1996; Merttens and Newland, 1996; Merttens et al., 1996; Schellekens, 1998; Topping and Bamford, 1988). Much of the available evidence comes from the IMPACT project and we have commented earlier on the problem of a lack of a rigorous programmatic evaluation of this major initiative. The consequence is that the evidence of participation and positive attitudes on the part of participating families tends to be stronger than the evidence of gains in attainment – though the latter kind of evidence does indeed exist.

An important characteristic of the IMPACT project is that it has sought to build into its structures and processes the relationship between parental involvement schemes and the marginalisation of family cultures which we noted in discussing literacy projects (Border and Merttens, 1993; Merttens, 1996). The IMPACT solution appears to be to avoid requiring parents to take on the role of **teachers** of their children, which in turn would require them to accept the norms and presuppositions associated with that role. Instead, parents act as **partners** with their children in shared activities without being required to transmit knowledge or information in any formalised manner. This appears partly to resolve the cultural imperialism issue and enables parents from different social and cultural backgrounds to participate on similar terms. However, as Merttens herself accepts, it does not address directly the issue of non-participation.

Other forms of parental involvement

The overwhelming bulk of the evidence available on the effects of parental involvement in children's learning relates to the 'basic skills' of literacy and numeracy. Where evidence relating to the remainder of the curriculum is forthcoming, it may still retain a 'basic skills' focus (City and County of Swansea Community Outdoor Education Service, 1996, 1997, 1998), or relate to the positive effects pre-school 'preparation for learning' activities by parents (Bastiani, 1997; Hinton, 1989). We have been able to find almost nothing which deals with parental involvement in subjects of the curriculum other than literacy and numeracy.

Not surprisingly, therefore, there is relatively little which deals with parental involvement in children's learning in the secondary phase, and what there is may continue to focus on 'the basics'. However, the limited literature in this field does point to a replication of the sorts of positive effects on attainments and attitudes that are found at

primary level (Capper *et al.*, 1998; Frater, 1997; Mayall, 1990; Sandler, 1989).

Dissident views

For the most part, the literature on parental involvement in learning presents such involvement as an unequivocal good. The concern, by and large, is to describe what has been done in promoting involvement and to demonstrate its effectiveness in raising attainments. However, as we have already seen in looking at the literature on literacy and numeracy, there are dissident voices. These tend to focus on the assumptions built into the parental involvement 'movement'. First, there are some doubts as to whether many teachers value parental involvement as highly as many of its advocates in the literature (Hancock, 1998; Long, 1993). This is partly due to the practical constraints under which teachers operate (most schools, for instance, are not resourced specifically for parental outreach), and partly due to the threat that parents might pose to the role of teachers as guardians of the curriculum and experts in learning.

Second, there are doubts about whether teachers fully understand and value the diversity of families (Crozier, 1998; Edwards and David, 1997; Maclachlan, 1996). The evidence here seems to suggest that the attempt to involve parents in learning more fully is premised on the assumptions that parents (and, particularly, mothers) should relate to their children in particular ways and that some of them (particularly from working class or ethnic minority groups) fail to comply with this norm. Both of these assumptions are questionable on ethical and empirical grounds and the failure of teachers to question them may lead them both to devalue the contribution such families can (and do) make to children's learning and to alienate them further from their children's schools.

Summary

The literature on parental involvement in learning is the most substantial and, in some ways, most sophisticated in the area of school-family-community links. It offers convincing evidence that involving parents in their children's learning is likely to enhance the attainments of children, to improve their attitudes to learning and to be welcomed by many parents.

The literature is particularly strong on parental involvement in literacy and, to a lesser extent, in numeracy. It is much weaker in other areas of the curriculum and somewhat so in the secondary phase where the full curriculum takes on added importance. However, what evidence there is points to the benefits of parental involvement.

On the other hand, there are some caveats to be entered. The literature is, in particular, somewhat success-oriented and we know too little about 'failures' in this field. Not all schemes are equally successful for all parents and children – but we do not fully understand why. Similarly, we know very little about the schools, teachers and, in particular, parents who drop out of schemes or do not participate in the first instance. There are also ethical and political issues around this area. The model of parent-child relations and of family values embedded in the parental involvement movement may well operate as a form of cultural imperialism, devaluing the practices and values of families who may already be somewhat marginalised. The net effect may simply be to alienate those families and disadvantage their children further.

4 Parents as partners

In addition to the direct involvement of parents in children's learning activities, schools attempt to work with parents in a range of ways which we deal with here under the umbrella term of 'parents as partners'. These ways include school support for families, school-home communication and parents' help for schools.

School support for families

It is a relatively small step, at least in the current literature on school-family-community links, from schools' attempting to involve parents in their children's learning to their offering direct support to families. Reporting a parent support programme in Liverpool, for instance, Davis (1989) describes the connection in the following way:

> The notion of supporting parents is but one of the facets of a more general movement of parent involvement, and behind it there is clearly the idea that in the present climate the education system needs their support. (256)

In other words, schools offer direct support to families and, in return, parents are in a better position to offer support to the work of schools (Alexander, 1997). Ideally, both sides of the partnership gain from this arrangement, though there is, of course, potential for tension between them – an issue to which we shall return.

Despite the evident attractions of this model and the proliferation of school-family support projects on the ground, the quality of the evidence in this area is low. For the most part, the literature comprises reports on local projects, frequently written by the professionals leading the project and usually evaluated (if at all) in terms of stakeholder satisfaction and participation rates. As Whyte (1997) points out, there are real difficulties in evaluating such projects where they do not establish specific indicators of success and measures of children's social and academic development. We might add that evaluation becomes even more problematic where the aims of projects are wide-ranging (a generalised 'support to families') and where indicators of success are therefore difficult to establish.

Nonetheless, there are some things we can say even on the basis of this limited evidence. Some projects identify a specific and practical form of support that schools (often with other partners) can offer to families. This might, for instance, take the form of childcare facilities in or out of schools (Dench and O'Regan, 1998; Education Extra, 1997a; Gatenby, 1998), or transport to school for children living in a multiply-disadvantaged area (Save the Children, 1996). In each of these cases, the support was appreciated by families and, in the latter case particularly, brought benefits to schools that were involved in terms of increased attendance and punctuality together with improved behaviour. These schemes, however, tended to depend on external funding, so that their long-term sustainability must be in doubt if that funding were to be withdrawn.

Other projects similarly target a specific problem in school for which increased support to families is seen as a solution. This may take the form of a support group for parents who are reluctant to become involved with schools (Kahn and Sugden, 1995), or support to refugee families (Vincent and Warren, 1998b), or support to families at the point of their children's entry into primary school (Whyte, 1997), or work with parents whose children are at risk of (disciplinary) exclusion

(George, 1998; Hayden, 1997) or who are not attending school regularly (Bryce, 1999; Irving and Parker-Jenkins, 1995) or who are in danger of drifting into criminality (Graham, 1998).

A third group of projects aim at developing parenting skills or at a more generalised 'trouble-shooting' service for families (Grimshaw and McGurie, 1998; Guishard, 1998; Liverpool Parent School Partnership, 1996; Malek, 1996; Sheffield LEA, 1998; Vincent and Warren, 1998a; Wolfendale, 1998). In these and many other projects, it is not uncommon for schools to work in close partnership with other agencies who have the skills and resources to work directly with families.

The evaluations which emerge from these projects are broadly positive, in that the projects appear to be workable and support is offered by them that appears to be both needed and appreciated. However, there are some underlying tensions and ambiguities. At a practical level, the sustainability of schools' offering support to families is severely constrained by the lack of specific funding for this purpose and the other pressing imperatives which schools have to obey. In practice, headteachers, particularly in multiply-disadvantaged areas, spend a good deal of time in quasi-social-work activities with families and find this to be a considerable strain (Webb and Vulliamy, 1996). It is hardly surprising, therefore, that many of the initiatives reported in the literature arise out of externally-funded projects rather than practices which are fully embedded within schools; as Bastiani (1991) suggests, home-school partnerships may be too large and complex for schools to manage alone. There may, moreover, be particular difficulties where schools attempt to work with more problematic families where there is a good deal of turbulence such that long-term partnerships

become difficult to establish (Hayden, 1997)

Further, the issue of cultural imperialism is as prominent here as in the field of parental involvement in learning. Whatever the practices of schemes and the attitudes of individual professionals, it is remarkable how many of them reflect the priorities of schools and teachers – which may or may not be the priorities of parents. In fact, as Vincent and Warren (1998a) point out, parenting courses and other forms of support, tend simultaneously both to be valued by parents and to run the risk of imposing one social group's view of 'good parenting' on another. Similarly, other commentators (Edwards and Knight, 1994; Grimshaw and McGurie, 1998) highlight the lack of clarity over the aims of support for families and the potential for conflicting interpretations both between parents and schools and between schools and other agencies.

The ambiguity is perhaps best illustrated in the report by Malek (1996) cited above which states on the same page that the 'central rule' of the family support project in question is that '"it puts the interests of the child first"' and yet that the activities undertaken 'are based on the needs of individual schools, they therefore vary from school to school' (3). Given this ambiguity, it is not difficult to see how the 'interests of the child' might be reinterpreted to coincide with the 'needs of the school'.

Edwards and Knight (1994) draw a broad but useful distinction between what they call 'needy parents' and 'parents as consumers'. The latter are those articulate and resourceful parents who can act as customers of the education service and can demand that schools operate in ways which satisfy them. The former are those parents whose difficulties and disadvantages make them the target of support from, and turn them into the clients of, schools and other agencies. Certainly, the studies available in the literature overwhelmingly relate to schools in multiply-disadvantaged areas and are targeted at 'needy parents'. This in itself may be neither surprising nor undesirable but what makes it particularly concerning is that we can find little evidence in the literature that parental support is based on any thorough investigation of the actual circumstances of families, the parenting practices within them (including what may be very positive features of those practices) or on any genuinely collaborative attempt at needs analysis. That some of the needs of some parents are being met by such schemes seems beyond doubt. However, the question remains as to whether the needs of schools may not sometimes take precedence over the needs of families.

School-home communication

In an important sense, any form of link between school and home involves communication. However, there is a small literature which deals explicitly with the more formal mechanisms which schools establish to keep parents informed about their children's progress. In terms of future directions for policy and practice, there are two developments reported positively in this literature. The first is the involvement of parents in the educational assessment of their children (Wolfendale, 1988, 1993, 1995), on the grounds that parents can bring to bear a range of detailed knowledge across a range of contexts and over many years, which professionals cannot hope to match.

The second is the emergence of a range of 'bridges' between home and school which attempt to ensure that the gulf between parents and teachers is not so wide as it otherwise might be. These can take the form of personnel, such as home-school liaison coordinators attached to schools (McNamara *et al.*, 1992; Vincent, 1996b), of facilities such as parents centres where parents and professionals can meet (Davis, 1989; Gale, 1996; Philips, 1989; Vincent, 1996b), of new forms of communication (such as videos about the school made by pupils and distributed to parents (Hancock *et al.*, 1996)), or more formalised agreements and contracts between home and school (Bastiani, 1996a; Macbeth, 1993). One particularly creative project, for instance, rejected the conventional notion of parenting courses as overly-patronising and instead involved parents in an urban primary school in making a video about child development, using the school's nursery as a case study (Hunt and Robson, 1998).

In each case, the literature has something positive to say about these initiatives. Given the somewhat limited scope of home-school communications in many schools, developments such as these mark a clear advance and are enthusiastically presented (often by their originators or sponsors). As we shall see in the next chapter, parents tend to be somewhat keener on learning more about what is happening to their child in school and informing the school about their child's needs and wishes than on more formal involvement in governance and management.

However, the literature is also somewhat ambivalent about school-home communication in general. A number of commentators (Brown, 1993; Crozier, 1996; Vincent, 1996a, 1996b; Vincent and Tomlinson, 1998; Walker, 1998a, 1996b) point out that, despite the eagerness of many parents for genuine dialogue, such communication tends, in practice, to be dominated by teachers and allied professionals. However promising particular initiatives may look as ways of opening up channels of communication, teachers and other professionals tend to control those channels, the (educational) language through which communication is mediated, and the decision-making which communication is intended to inform. They tend, moreover, to be reluctant to loosen their grip on this control and to be particularly defensive in dealing with parents from, for instance, ethnic minorities, who do not neatly fit into their stereotypical notions of 'good' parents. Although some commentators emphasise the importance of personal qualities and relationships in promoting good communication (Adams *et al.*, 1994; Marsh, 1994; Strahan, 1994), it is difficult to see how this person-centred approach can do more than ameliorate the structural barriers which underlie it.

Parents' help for schools

There is a similarly small literature which focuses on the help which parents and other community members can offer to schools. Although the use of parent helpers in schools has been widespread, the only study of their effectiveness we have identified is by Thomas (1992), who makes useful points about the need for clarity of role definition and for training for teachers in how to work with helpers. Elliott (1998) similarly describes an accredited training course for parent helpers which appears to have been much appreciated by the parents involved.

Beyond this, the literature echoes much of what we have already reviewed in identifying a tendency for teachers to protect their own status and power by marginalising the contribution that parents

might make. Reporting on practice in early years provision, where parents are stereotypically held to be at their most proactive, for instance, Smith (1988) states that they are, for the most part, involved in 'servicing' schools (making and mending equipment, fundraising and so on) rather than in working directly with children or in managing provision.

Special needs education

There are many specific contexts for parent partnership which could be analysed in greater depth. Early years education and education in multi-ethnic communities, for instance, are two areas where the issues raised more generally above take on particular salience. However, we have opted instead to highlight special needs education for the reason that parent-school-professional relations in that field are governed by distinctive legislation. Since the 1981 Education Act, parents have had rights to an input into decision-making about their children's educational future, which have been significantly strengthened in recent years. Moreover, this field has seen the emergence of a series of powerful parental pressure groups aiming both at supporting parents in the decision-making process and making an input into policy development. The question is whether this legislative framework has altered the essential features of parental partnership which we have described elsewhere.

The answer would seem to be that, to some extent, it has. It is possible, for instance, to point to a range of developments in special needs education – Parent Partnership Schemes (Daly, 1999; Wolfendale, 1997b), early intervention initiatives (Hornby, 1995), specialist interventions which demand a high level of parental input (Sutton, 1998; Thomas, 1993) and the emergence of parental lobby groups outside the normal educational decision-making system (Tomlinson and Vincent, 1997) – as examples of what can be achieved when the somewhat tentative forms of partnership are supported by legislation, funding and clear prioritisation.

However, here, as elsewhere, there are tensions. For all the statutory and other support available to parents, professionals continue to maintain substantial control of the partnership process (Armstrong, 1995; Calliste, 1993; Sandow, Stafford, and Stafford, 1987) and schools continue to see 'partnership' as something which need not (or cannot) concern them too closely (Wolfendale, 1997b). The direct intervention of government, in other words, appears to have been successful in altering the surface features of school and family links in the field of special needs education, but not in changing its deep structures.

Dissident voices

As was the case in parental involvement in learning, much of the literature on parent partnership is concerned to report projects and initiatives intended to improve the current state of affairs. It is not surprising, therefore, that much of it concentrates (quite properly) on the successes of these initiatives. However, it will be evident from problematic issues that we have raised throughout this chapter that there is a 'dissident view' of parental partnership which is perhaps even stronger here than in the field of parental involvement in learning.

As Macbeth (1995) points out, the concept of partnership is ambiguous, meaning different things to different stakeholders. Certainly, this is true of schools and parents and it is not surprising, therefore, that there is considerable variation in partnership practices with a good deal of hesitancy on both sides of the relationship (Johnston, 1996) and differences even within the parent body as to what sort of partnership is desirable (Brighouse, 1993). Under these circumstances, it is inevitable that, even in areas such as early years provision, where the rhetoric of partnership is at its most powerful, the reality should have fallen some way short of that rhetoric (Pugh, 1989).

Moreover, there seems to be an underlying explanatory factor that accounts for many of these difficulties. Bastiani (1989a) underlines the points we have seen made by other commentators, arguing that parent-school partnership takes place very much on the professional's terms, is conceptualised through professional ideology and articulated through professional language. Under these circumstances, many parents experience such 'partnership' in terms of 'inequality, social distance and powerlessness' (181) (see also Todd and Higgins, 1998). It follows that moves to involve parents as partners in schools can equally well be read as moves to control the relationship between schools and parents (Tomlinson and Vincent, 1997) and, indeed, there is some evidence of parents' being systematically marginalised when they are perceived by professionals as threats to their ability to control the relationship (Morgan *et al.*, 1993). There are further charges that this phenomenon is particularly marked in ethnically and culturally diverse areas where the predominantly white and middle class culture of the teaching profession marginalises large groups of parents by failing to recognise their diversity (Vincent, 1995).

The literature is not strong on evidence as to how and where this imbalance between professionals and parents might be overcome. The most obvious response, of legislating for more equal relationships, does not seem to be completely effective – as the case of special needs education demonstrates. However, the literature does offer some examples (Tomlinson and Vincent, 1997; Vincent and Warren, 1999) of parents' groups which operate on the education system but outside the controlling influence of education professionals. It may be that such groups offer, not so much an alternative to partnership, but an alternative power base from which parents can engage with professionals.

Summary

In addition to involving parents directly in their children's learning, the education service in general and schools in particular seek to develop a partnership with parents in a range of ways: through offering support to families, through enhancing their communications with parents and through enlisting the help of parents for schools themselves. There is evidence that each of these forms of partnership produces positive effects, not least in that it is appreciated and valued by parents. There is particular evidence from the field of special needs education, where relationships have been placed on a more formal and statutory footing, that such formalisation is effective in requiring the education service to engage fully with parents.

However, the evidence in this field has some limitations, not least because evaluation of the effects of more extended partnerships is difficult and because the literature tends to focus on local initiatives, sometimes sponsored by the bodies which also commission the research or evaluation. Moreover, there is some evidence that the development of partnerships imposes strains on schools who have to manage such partnerships alongside their other priorities. This may explain why many of the initiatives reported in the literature tend to be funded and led from outside the (individual) school.

More fundamentally, the literature demonstrates an underlying power imbalance between education professionals and parents. Partnership takes place very much on terms dictated by the former, with the consequent marginalisation of the latter – an issue which may be particularly important where parents belong to social groups that already experience marginalisation. There is little indication in the literature as to how this issue might be addressed, though there is some limited evidence of parental groups operating successfully outside the direct control of education professionals.

5 The school and the community

It is probably true to say that the bulk of the literature on school-family-community links focuses on the first two terms in that three-part equation. Not only is the notion of 'community' notoriously ambiguous and open to differing interpretations (Fielding, 1996; Vincent, 1993), but it is, in practical terms, easier for schools to develop relationships with a finite body of parents than with a nebulous 'community' – many of whose children may, in any case, attend different schools. Nonetheless, there is a literature on schools and communities, and we propose to review it here in terms of three distinct but interrelated strands – collaborations between schools and other 'community agencies' (which we have interpreted broadly as statutory and voluntary service-providers, local business and industry, community groups and so on), community education and the involvement of the community in educational decision-making and the management of the school.

Collaboration with community agencies

To a certain extent, some of the dimensions of collaboration with community agencies are already well-known. Many of the initiatives reported in earlier chapters involve joint working between teachers, other professionals and community groups and the comments made on those initiatives apply equally here. Moreover, there is a substantial and well-established literature on inter-agency collaboration which provides a useful framework (see Dyson *et al*, 1998, for a review). This literature points to the very real possibilities of collaboration, particularly where professionals share a common purpose (self-generated or defined by legislation), where they are able to work in joint teams or

shared centres and where they are able to build up trust over time. However, it also points to endemic problems in collaboration stemming from the different (and often conflicting) legislative frameworks within which the statutory agencies work, the different priorities they establish and definitions of 'need' which govern their work, and the different professional cultures which arise from the different bases of their work and professional training they receive.

Beyond these well-rehearsed findings, however, the literature reveals an important educational role for collaboration with community agencies. If we regard the 'core business' of schools as being the delivery of the prescribed curriculum (a substantial part of which is the National Curriculum), then the positive role which emerges for non-education professionals is at the periphery (in a non-pejorative sense) of that curriculum. This role seems to take two major forms. The first is to do with provision for vulnerable and disaffected children and young people, where some additional form of support appears to be a prerequisite of their being educated in a more conventional sense. The role of the other statutory agencies for such children who have special educational needs is well-established (Dyson *et al.*, 1998). However, there is good evidence in the literature for the effectiveness of collaborative work with other groups such as those at risk of exclusion, or whose behaviour is causing concern, or who are experiencing personal and family turbulence (Anderson *et al.*, 1995; Dasgupta and Richards, 1997; Fitzherbert and Yeo, 1997; George, 1998; Hayden, 1997; Lloyd, 1994; Samson and Hart, 1995; Utting, 1996; Vernon and Sinclair, 1998; Wetz, 1996).

Such collaborations are not without their difficulties, which seem to stem ultimately from the well-known barriers to collaboration outlined above (see, for instance, Armstrong and Moon, 1993; Atkins *et al*, 1996; Lindsay *et al*, 1998). However, where they are effective, that effectiveness appears to stem from the capacity of other partners to 'add value' to a school's efforts – and vice versa. In particular, agencies beyond the school are able to mediate between home and school and hence to address some of the causal factors underlying children's difficulties in a way that schools alone find difficult. It may be – though this can be no more than speculation – that because the aims of the initiative are not clearly part of the core business of schools, there is less tendency on the part of schools to retain control of initiatives and redefine them in terms of their own priorities. It may also be that some of these initiatives, at least, are founded on good research evidence and are not simply the product of school-level creativity.

The second aspect of the 'peripheral' role of collaboration is in the delivery of those aspects of the curriculum which are not simply academic. There is, for instance, evidence for the effectiveness of multi-disciplinary health and drugs education programmes (Hurry and Lloyd, 1997; Jamieson, 1998; Lowden and Powney, 1994, 1995, 1996; Shiner and Newburn, 1996), of anti-bullying and other antisocial-behaviour initiatives (Bell and Sigsworth, 1992; Crime Concern, 1998a, b, c; Smith, 1997), and of a range of other initiatives involving non-teachers in an educational role or setting (Black *et al*, 1992; Hand and Wright, 1997; Howieson and Semple, 1996; Kushner, 1991; Taylor, 1991).

Again, it is important not to minimise the difficulties faced by such collaborations. There is evidence, for instance, of inter-professional distrust and conflict (HMI, 1990; Jeffs and Smith, 1991,

1998) and some of the studies cited above report difficulties faced by schools both in incorporating initiatives into the 'core' of their work and in finding the time and funds to sustain links. Nonetheless, the widely reported positive effects are difficult to ignore. Again, the explanation may be that schools are less possessive of these 'peripheral' activities than of core activities (such as the teaching of reading), that most initiatives are externally resourced and led and that they frequently draw on good experience and evidence.

An additional explanatory factor is hinted at by Shiner and Newburn (1996) in attempting to account for the relative effectiveness of peer-led programmes for drugs education. They argue that effectiveness is largely determined by the 'credibility' of the programme leader. Such credibility, they suggest, can be person-based (derived from personal characteristics), experience-based (derived from the experiences which the leader is able to recount) or message-based (derived from the message delivered by the leader). While each of these forms of credibility is important, Shiner and Newburn suggest that experience-based credibility, provided it is accompanied by message-based credibility, is the most significant. The apparent successes of many programmes involving non-teachers in 'peripheral' areas, therefore, may be due to their possession of a degree of credibility, arising from a breadth of experience outside the education system, which is necessarily denied to teachers.

This may also go some way towards explaining the apparent successes of a further type of partnership – that is, partnership with business and industry. This success is not unequivocal. The development of education-business partnerships appears to have been somewhat patchy due, at least in part, to the lack of consistent year-on-year funding base (Bowen and Bennett, 1998). It also appears to have had a patchy impact on schools and, particularly, on pupils. Such partnerships impact on the culture of schools where they have been coherently thought-through and taken seriously by all partners, but are also prey to limited participation and lack of coherence (Bowen and Bennett, 1998; QPID, 1997; Turner *et al.*, 1994; Wilson *et al.*, 1996). Moreover, there is some evidence that the problem lies with the difficulties schools have had in understanding the potential contribution of industry and incorporating that contribution into their core business (Hillage, 1995; Warwick, 1995).

On the other hand, there is some good evidence that links such as compacts and mentoring can have benefits for both parties, and particularly for young people themselves (Chaplain and Gray, 1999; Day and Kannike, 1999; Golden and Sims, 1997; Miller, 1997; Saunders and Morris, 1995; Schagen, 1997). There is some variability in the extent to which these benefits are delivered by particular programmes, but it does appear that such programmes can be effective in improving motivation, attendance and, ultimately, attainment. The clarity of the programme's aims, selection criteria and definition of roles appear to be crucial factors in determining this effectiveness. It also seems that where school-business and -industry links form part of an overall package of curriculum modification, learning support and inter-agency support, there is some limited evidence that they might impact positively on the motivation and retention rates of disaffected older students (DfEE, 1996; Kinder and Wilkin, 1998; Kinder *et al.*, 1999).

Again, the notion of credibility may be useful in partly explaining the impact of business partnerships, mentoring and work experience. It seems reasonable to suppose that some young people – particularly if they are already disaffected from schooling – may grant only limited credibility to their teachers when they try to inform them about the world beyond school. Non-educationalists may, on the other hand, be granted much more credibility and may be able to relate the learning process and school itself to that wider world in a way that teachers, by virtue of their role, find difficult.

An interesting and recent subset of the literature in this field has been generated by the current government's 'crusade for standards' and is concerned with maximising the opportunities for children to learn through summer schools and other forms of out-of-hours learning (Basic Skills Agency, 1998; Education Extra, 1997b, c; Prince's Trust, 1997, 1998; Sainsbury *et al.*, 1998). While there are early indications of some limited effectiveness of these approaches, there has been no opportunity as yet for long-term evaluation and there is a tendency in the available literature to confuse enthusiastic description (for the purposes of dissemination) with rigorous evaluation (for the purposes of policy development).

It is perhaps worth adding that, in general terms, the quality of the research and evaluation evidence in this field is somewhat higher than in other areas of the school-family-community literature which we have reviewed. This may be coincidence, or may be a consequence of many initiatives in this area being led by (non-education) organisations which are accustomed to (and have the resources for) commissioning high-quality and independent evaluation. On the other hand, it is also worth noting that the powerful and illuminating critical literature which has informed most other areas we have reviewed appears to be absent here. Important political and ethical issues are raised by both the vocationalisation of the curriculum and by offering highly disadvantaged young people mentors who (whatever their backgrounds) are now highly 'successful'. However, these issues are not discussed in the evaluative literature.

Community education

If the critical literature is missing in the field of collaboration with community agencies, it makes its presence more fully felt in respect of community education. As Vincent (1993) points out, community education is something of a 'forgotten area' which had a 'brief flowering' (1) in the 1970s – and before that, of course, in the pre-war Cambridgeshire community colleges – but which has largely disappeared from the education agenda as a result of the market-oriented reforms of the 1980s. Not surprisingly, therefore, there is little evaluative literature in this field (Jeffs, 1992).

The majority of the literature that exists, however, is concerned with an ideological debate regarding the nature of community and the possibility of genuinely community-oriented and community-owned education (Clark, 1992, 1996; Duncan, 1989; Fielding, 1996; Fletcher and Bramley, 1996; Jeffs, 1992; Monck and Husbands, 1996; O'Hagen, 1991; Tomlinson, 1991; Vincent, 1993; Watt, 1989). Although different commentators adopt somewhat different positions, the general outline of the debate is clear. It starts from the premise that the notion of community is highly problematic. It is not simply that traditional images of homogeneous communities no longer hold good, but that such simplistic images can be

used by the policy-makers, managers and teachers who control the education system to avoid relinquishing that control by engaging with the actual diversity and real needs of communities. Community education tends, therefore, to be 'bolted on' to existing school provision, practice and policy rather than becoming embedded within it and generating its own internal dynamic to change schools. This situation is exacerbated by the education reforms of the 1980s which foreground the notion of parents as individual consumers of the education 'product', thus substituting the aggregation of such individual consumers for any notion of an overarching community interest. Under these circumstances, there is no effective way for community members to exert influence on the education system collectively and no inclination on the part of education professionals to enter into genuine partnership with them.

Within this somewhat gloomy picture, there is a good deal of advocacy of what might be done to generate a community voice in education – but rather little evidence of what has been done effectively. There is, for instance, some limited evidence of the beneficial effects (but heavy demands) of including adults in mainstream classes (Blair *et al.*, 1995), some evidence that schools offering community education can successfully enlist their adult students in supporting the learning of young children (Newton, 1998), some indications of the possibilities for a community role for rural schools (Bell and Sigsworth, 1992; Mills, 1992), some ideas for how the curriculum might become more community-oriented (Brighouse, 1991; Howe and Wilson, 1995) and an unevaluated outline of an alternative structure of governance for community schools (Giles, 1992). Otherwise, we are able to confirm Jeffs' (1992) conclusion that, in the literature of the last ten years, there is no substantial body of research and evaluation into effects and effectiveness. However, we note with interest a proposal in a conference paper by Fletcher and Bramley (1996) for a multi-strand and multi-level model of evaluation for community schools and shall return to this in the final chapter.

Decision-making and management

Many of the issues which arise in the field of community education are also apparent in respect of the involvement of families and communities in decision-making and management in schools. Munn (1998) usefully categorises involvement into three types: the involvement of parents as consumers exercising their right to choose a school for their child; the direct involvement of parents and community members as school governors; and the impact of parents and community members on policy through single- or multiple-issue educational lobbying organisations. Much research and debate in this field centres around the implications of the education reforms of the 1980s and early 1990s (notably, the 1988 Education Reform Act) for each of these forms of involvement – and, particularly, for the first two.

Although there is some ambivalence in the literature about the notion of parental choice – largely on the grounds that it does indeed introduce an element of accountability to parents that was previously absent (Beresford, 1992; Thomas, 1989) – the research evidence suggests that consumerism has not delivered the sort of control over schools which might have been imagined. Partly, this is because parents with different characteristics and in different social circumstances are likely to want

different things from schools and to have different possibilities for exercising real choice; partly it is because schools do not respond to the market situation by listening in great detail to the wants and needs of individual parent-consumers but rather by devising strategies to maximise their own market advantage – which may mean appealing to particular sectors of the market or 'selling' the school as it is (Ball, 1993; Ball, Bowe, and Gewirtz, 1996; Gewirtz, Ball, and Bowe, 1995; Munn, 1993, 1998; Reay and Ball, 1997, 1998; Vincent, 1996; Woods, 1996). Moreover, there is some evidence that many parents would prefer something more akin to a partnership with schools – the enhanced communication to which we referred in the previous chapter – rather than the producer-consumer relationship which the market imposes (Hughes, 1993; Hughes *et al.*, 1994).

The research evidence on governors is no more encouraging. While the education reforms of the 1980s and 1990s significantly increased the notional powers of governors, particularly relative to those of headteachers (Ribbens, 1989), the reality seems to be that governors tend to defer to education professionals rather than articulating a distinctive parental or community voice, unless there is some specific issue (such as threatened school closure) which energises them (Golby *et al.*, 1989; Munn, 1998; Thody, 1995).

In terms of lobby groups operating outside the statutory systems of governance and choice, Munn (1998) concludes that, while they have an impact on peripheral policy issues, they rarely influence core policy decisions. We might add that there are also issues about which parents and community members become involved in such groups and how far they are capable of involving the most disadvantaged (an issue of particular salience in special needs education (Dyson, 1997, 1998; Riddell, Brown, and Duffield, 1994). We have, however, already seen some suggestions that these offer an alternative pathway to genuine power (Tomlinson and Vincent, 1997) and there are additionally a few examples both of direct action by communities (Carspecken, 1991) and of local structures which act as a counterbalance to the statutory bodies and processes (Giles, 1992; Templeton, 1989). However, the overall conclusion has to be that, although the current mechanisms for parental and community involvement in governance and decision-making offer some opportunities for some groups to make a real impact on schools, they do not offer a means whereby communities as a whole can engage effectively with their schools.

Holistic approaches and community regeneration

Thus far, we have treated the different forms of school-family-community links as though they were entirely separate. This is convenient for analytical purposes and, to some extent, represents the situation on the ground, particularly where such links arise out of single-strand projects. However, there are two ways in which this analysis diverges from the reality of schools' relationships with their wider environment. The first is that all schools have, in fact, to manage each strand of family and community links in the context of every other strand; even a tightly-focused programme for involving parents in their children's reading, for instance, will be nested within a set of wider relationships with parents and community and will be influenced by them. This creates a particular challenge for evaluating the effectiveness of

particular initiatives and goes some way towards explaining why strategies that are effective in one context may not be so in another.

The second divergence is that some examples of linkage are deliberately constructed as part of a more holistic 'package' of relationships in order to generate a multi-strand approach to multi-dimensional problems. For the most part, the literature in this field is concerned with schools in disadvantaged areas. It would be unlikely in such areas that a more limited approach could be effective in overcoming either the multiple disadvantages experienced by children or the multiple barriers between families, communities and the schools which serve them (Barber and Dann, 1996; Barber *et al.*, 1996; DIECEC, 1998; Easen *et al.*, 1996; Hall *et al.*, 1992; Houston, 1996; NCOE, 1996; Liverpool Parent School Partnership, 1996; Wolfendale, 1996).

Although the issues raised by such approaches are essentially the same as those which arise from their component parts, they do have some distinctive features. In particular, there are issues to do with the coherence, impact and prospects for evaluation of such approaches. There is, for instance, considerable potential for different understandings of their aims and methods to arise among different stakeholders; an umbrella project may shelter a multitude of different interests and assumptions. There are also issues around developing a management structure which gives coherence to the overall approach without unduly constraining individual strands or contributors (Bridgwood, 1996).

In these respects, the work of the DIECEC (Developing Intercultural Education through Cooperation between European Cities) network is interesting. DIECEC has developed an illuminating notion of 'scaffolding' children's learning through 'multi-level working' (DIECEC, 1998, pp. 14 -15). In broad terms, this refers to developing a support structure for learning by working not only with children and young people themselves, but also with parents or carers, the community and a range of community agencies. Because the specification of levels is undertaken with some care, DIECEC is able to offer a framework for similar multi-strand initiatives. Moreover, it is keen to emphasise the role of monitoring and (internal) evaluation, which again promises to add coherence and – as we shall see in the next chapter – also offers interesting indicators as to how external evaluation might be undertaken in this complex field.

It is a short step from the multi-strand approaches described here to treating school-family-community links as part of wider regeneration initiatives. The literature here is not extensive (DETR, 1997; Gledhill, 1995; Social Exclusion Unit, 1998) and relies as much on optimistic description and exhortation as on hard evidence of effects and effectiveness. Moreover, the specific strategies that are advocated tend to be assembled from those which we have described under different headings elsewhere in this review. There is no evidence, therefore, of the emergence of distinctive education strands within coherent regeneration initiatives where the effectiveness of both the strategy as a whole and of its educational components has been unequivocally demonstrated. However, this link to regeneration demonstrates the possibility that educational initiatives can serve wider social and economic purposes.

Community diversity

This may be an appropriate point to add a note relating to a theme which cuts across all the literature on school-family-community links. Families and communities are, of course, of very diverse kinds. Sometimes in the literature, aspects of this diversity are addressed directly. For instance, we have just been considering strategies which seem particularly appropriate for communities experiencing multiple disadvantages. Similarly, there is a small subset of the literature which considers issues of ethnic diversity (see, for instance, Brehony, 1995; Crozier, 1996; Curle, 1993; Duncan, 1989; Hirst, 1998; Lyle *et al.*, 1996; Stoker, 1996; Tomlinson, 1993; Vincent and Warren, 1998, 1999; Wei, 1993).

Insofar as the literature deals in any detail with community and family diversity, its principal concern is with the way in which some communities and families experience a greater distance between themselves and the schools which their children attend than do others. The implication is that where there are significant ethnic, cultural and social divides between schools, families and communities, schools and their partners in LEAs and other agencies have to work that much harder to bridge those divides. What does not emerge is that those divides can necessarily be interpreted as meaning a lack of interest on the part of families and communities for education, nor that strategies which are different in kind (as opposed to degree) are called for.

However, conclusions in this area have to be tentative since there is a dearth of studies which compare the differential impact of strategies across different family and community contexts. Indeed, it is probably true to say that the dominance of the literature by professional concerns means that issues of family and community diversity are relatively under-researched. This is an area, therefore, where more work might prove very illuminating.

Summary

The possibilities and pitfalls of collaboration between community agencies are well-known and schools' involvements in such collaborations seem to share the same characteristics, not least of which are the professional misunderstandings and mistrust which characterise this area. However, there is evidence that non-educationalists can make an effective contribution to activities which lie at the 'periphery' of schools' work. In particular, they can contribute to work with vulnerable children, where they can mediate between schools and the child's family and community, and to the non-academic aspects of curriculum. There is also evidence that mentoring is effective in changing pupils' attitudes and raising their attainment. It may be that non-teachers bring with them a credibility arising from their experiences outside of school which teachers themselves cannot aspire to.

The situation with regard to community education and the participation of parents and community in school management and decision making is less positive. The education reforms of the late 1980s and early 1990s appear to have privileged individual parents acting as consumers over the community interest and have further marginalised those parents who, for whatever reason, are not able to exercise their consumer role effectively. As a result, there are real doubts as to whether community education meets the real needs of communities and whether communities are able to exert a real influence over the schools which serve them.

On the other hand, there is some evidence that, in areas experiencing multiple disadvantage, there is potential for schools to become involved in multi-strand initiatives aimed at addressing the multiple sources of disadvantage in a coherent way. There are problems about the coherence of such initiatives and the extent to which their effectiveness is proven, but they at least open up some interesting possibilities.

6 School-family-community links

In this chapter, we shall attempt to summarise our findings and to consider their implications first for research and then for policy and practice.

What do we know?

The evidence-base regarding school-family-community links is, as we have seen, less substantial and trustworthy than we might wish. Nonetheless, it does allow us to describe some features of the field with a fair degree of confidence:

• There are significant benefits available to schools for extending their links with families and communities. Their approaches are likely to be welcomed by many parents and community members and are likely to generate positive attitudes amongst both adults and the school's pupils. Where the links are targeted on raising children's attainment, there is a reasonable probability that they will be successful and a more detailed exploration of some of the literature cited here will reveal the specifics of how such initiatives can be conducted.

• On the other hand, even the best-researched and most carefully developed initiatives (in, say, parental involvement in literacy or business mentoring) do not come with absolute guarantees of effectiveness. Much seems to depend on the particulars of the implementation process and the characteristics of the partners – teachers, parents, pupils and others – who are involved. This is hardly surprising, given the complexities of the social systems where such interventions take place but it should alert us to the dangers of unreflective adoption of projects and schemes.

• One of the factors in the complexity of this area is that parent bodies and communities are not homogeneous – though they are often taken to be so. Initiatives tend to be predicated on models of family structures and parents' roles which do not fit every family and which can be alienating if imposed insensitively. In particular, it seems that parents are, by and large, much more willing to become involved in their children's education than they are often assumed to be and that this is a phenomenon which holds good across social classes and ethnic groups. However, there is a significant group of parents who are keen to work with schools but lack the skills or, more particularly, the confidence to offer their support. Efforts by schools targeted at this group are likely to pay rich dividends. Equally, there are parents who are alienated from schools, who may be particularly hard to reach and about whom we know relatively little. Attempts to work with this group may be more difficult, though there is some evidence that non-education professionals can mediate between schools and families where relationships are problematic.

• The development of extended links brings with it a cost for schools. Currently, schools are resourced and organised in order to carry out their 'core business' of curriculum delivery. Moving beyond this core business imposes additional burdens which some schools find unsustainable. It is no coincidence that a high proportion of projects and initiatives in the literature are resourced and led from beyond the school. This in turn, of course, carries with it the risk of such initiatives remaining peripheral to schools and of the short-termism that is associated with project funding.

- Despite the many positive features of school-family-community links, there are some endemic and significant problems. A theme running throughout this review is the tendency of teachers and other professionals to guard their positions of power and privilege in the education system. This is almost certainly not a conscious and deliberate act on the part of individuals, very many of whom are genuinely committed to the best interests of children and their families. However, the reality is that families and communities have few avenues through which they can exercise effective influence on the education system – a phenomenon which is particularly marked in the case of groups who are already marginalised. The consequence is that families and communities tend to play a somewhat peripheral role in the policies and practices of schools, welcome as helpers and supporters, but not as partners and decision-makers. Schools, therefore, tend to privilege their own and the education system's needs over the needs and wishes of parents and communities. Not only does this have major implications for the contribution which schools can make to their communities, but it means that schools systematically underestimate the resources that are available to them in their environments.

- A second endemic problem is the fragmented and localised nature of school-family-community links in the UK. The impression is that the field is characterised by a multiplicity of locally-led and locally-developed projects, replicating each other's discoveries and difficulties, but not systematised in any useful way. This is not unconnected to the multiplicity of often short-term funding sources (schools' delegated budgets, GEST funds, Standards Fund, LEA funds, TECs, City Challenge, SRB initiatives and so on) which support these projects. In turn, these features lead to the relatively low level of evidence generated by local evaluations.

What do we need to know?

- We are fortunate in having access to some interesting and illuminating evaluative studies, particularly in the field of parental involvement in learning. However, these tend to adopt experimental or quasi-experimental designs and therefore focus heavily on outcomes. We know much less about the processes which underpin those outcomes and this is a significant omission, given the variable effectiveness of the approaches in question. It is important that we understand not merely what effects particular approaches are likely to produce, but why they produce those effects and, equally important, under what circumstances they will fail so to do. Process-oriented studies are difficult to conduct because they involve engaging closely with the interactions of parents, children and teachers. They also involve a style of research different from that which some researchers in this field are accustomed to adopt. They may, therefore, involve substantial funding, an extended time-scale and partnerships between the current group of researchers and others who have specialisms in other fields – such as observational methods, socio-linguistics, child development and family studies.

- Similarly, we know little about those for whom standard approaches to parental involvement are ineffective – the drop-outs and non-participants who are absent from the majority of research studies as well as from the projects themselves. So long as the primary concern has been to demonstrate the effectiveness of parental involvement, such absentees have been of minimal importance. However, that effectiveness has been demonstrated to an acceptable level and it is important that we now understand more about those whose non-participation might doubly disadvantage their children. Again, a somewhat different style of research is needed from that which is apparent in much of the literature – a more ethnographic style which enables the voices of this silent group to be heard so that policies and practices can be formulated in the light of the needs and wishes of all parents.

- This, in fact, is merely a specific manifestation of a much wider phenomenon. Although the 'lay' voice is by no means entirely absent from the literature, it is striking how much research has been dominated by professional concerns and perspectives. This may not be unconnected with the fact that many researchers themselves have backgrounds as education professionals and, perhaps more significantly, that their work is – almost inevitably – commissioned and funded by education or other professionally-dominated bodies. The consequence is that we get only an incomplete sense from the literature of what families and communities want from schools, how they respond to school initiatives and how schools impact on their lives.

- Beyond this personal perspective, we have little information from the literature on the overall impacts of schools on their communities. While it is now commonplace to assert that poor schooling is characteristic of disadvantaged neighbourhoods

or that low educational attainment is a risk factor in social exclusion, it is much harder to find evidence in the literature we reviewed of the specific contributions of schools to the regeneration or decline of communities. Some of this evidence is very likely to be available in, say, the field of economics or social geography. However, given the potential, alluded to in the previous chapter, for schools to make a wider contribution to regeneration initiatives, there is an urgent need for these disparate bodies of literature to be brought together or for fresh research into these issues to be undertaken from a multi-disciplinary perspective.

- In the same vein, two interrelated but distinct research traditions can be identified in the literature we reviewed. On the one hand, there is a broadly evaluative tradition, concerned with identifying the effectiveness of particular projects and initiatives and demonstrating the outcomes that particular approaches can produce. On the other hand, there is a tradition of critical policy analysis which is concerned much more with the broader (and often unintended) effects of initiatives and with problematising the assumptions on which they are based. These two traditions are by no means unaware of each other's existence and there are some notable attempts to enable their concerns to illuminate one another (Merttens, *et al.*, 1993 being a particularly interesting example). However, there is need for a more sustained dialogue between these two traditions so that we have a better understanding of school-family-community links 'in the round'.

- Although we have some information on the

effects of various strategies for linking schools with families and communities, we have almost no information on cost-effectiveness. There are a number of reasons for this: different strategies are almost never compared with each other; most reports provide no information on the costs even of single strategies; and reports of effectiveness tend to focus on short-term outcomes rather than on the longer term where substantial savings (such as in the provision of supportive services) might be anticipated. It seems likely that the 'bolt-on' nature of much of the funding for work in this field discourages the sort of comparative and longitudinal approach to research which would be needed to make good this deficit, combined, perhaps, with a proper sense that rights and duties are involved in school-family-community links which are not susceptible to mechanistic costing procedures. Nonetheless, basic cost-effectiveness data is not difficult to generate and definitions of 'costs' and 'benefits' can be arrived at which acknowledge the wider issues involved. Work of this kind, moreover, may be an important means of justifying a shift of funding from its current project basis to a more stable mainstream position.

- This leads us to the wider question of the fragmentary and (often) low-level nature of research and evaluation in this field. Local evaluations of local projects are essential for the development of those projects and are frequently illuminating for projects elsewhere. They are particularly important given what we have said about the variability in the effectiveness of approaches across specific contexts. However, they form a poor basis on which to formulate large-scale (national, for example) policy or to generate

any sort of secure knowledge in this field. In fact, they manifest many of the alleged inadequacies for which educational research has been roundly criticised recently – though the fault seems to lie at least as much with the demands of research sponsors as with the predilections of education researchers. Nonetheless, it is important to raise the level of research in this field in at least three respects – its scale, its scope and its depth.

What we mean by the scale of research in this field is essentially to do with the number of cases with which a study deals, its time-scale and the extent to which single studies become part of an interconnecting network of studies (for example, by replicating each other in different contexts). Establishing convincing evidence as to the effectiveness or otherwise of particular approaches ultimately depends on obeying certain scientific disciplines – for adequate controls, for minimum sample sizes, for replication and for long-term follow-up – which simply cannot be applied to a multiplicity of small-scale, short-term studies based on non-identical approaches. Although such 'good' evidence may never amount to 'certain' proof, it is better than the 'best guesses' which characterise the field currently. It demands, however, significant research funding, evaluations which are planned into initiatives from the start and, above all, initiatives which are themselves sufficiently large-scale to generate the necessary data.

What we mean by the scope of the research is the extent to which it encompasses not simply single strand initiatives, but the totality of schools' family and community links, together with the broader education policy and socio-economic contexts within which those links are located. An endemic problem of effectiveness studies in complex contexts is that they find it difficult to disentangle the outcomes of the target initiative from the whole range of other factors at work in the situation. Even if they can do this, they cannot adequately trace the wider effects of that initiative beyond its immediate outcomes. Scope, in the sense we have defined it, therefore, is an essential complement to scale.

Similarly, depth is an essential complement to both scope and scale. By depth, we mean the capacity of a study to search beneath the surface features of a situation to its underlying processes. As we have indicated elsewhere, it is not enough to understand the likely effectiveness or even effects of an initiative if we cannot also understand how such effectiveness and effects are produced.

- The call for enhanced scale, scope and depth does not mean that all studies should be of the same type or should manifest each of these characteristics. However, it does mean that we need studies which make a significant contribution in one or more of these respects and, in particular, that the further proliferation of small-scale studies is unlikely to add much to what we already know. There is a need, therefore, for large-scale evaluative studies to meet the criterion of scale, for detailed case-studies to meet the criterion of depth and for 'multi-level' case studies to meet the criterion of scope. This last type of study is foreshadowed by the notion of multi-level evaluation (DIECEC, 1998) and by some of the ideas on the evaluation of community education put forward by Fletcher and Bramley

(1996). The key to such studies is that they locate the range of school-family-community links within a wider social and educational context, employing a range of quantitative and qualitatively-based methodologies at each level as appropriate.

- Given that we need a variety of research styles and methods, it is also important that research in this field is more programmatic than has hitherto been the case. In other words, we need studies which consciously build on one another, replicating each other's findings, problematising each other's assumptions and filling each other's gaps. It may be that this can be achieved through semi-formal means which encourage researchers to engage with each other – conferences, seminars, journals, edited volumes and the like. However, it may also demand a more formal programmatic approach in which major research sponsors with an interest in this field – DfEE (and through them, other government departments and the Social Exclusion Unit), ESRC and the Joseph Rowntree Foundation – combine to sponsor a well-structured and interrelated series of studies.

What can we do?

At local level:

- At school and local level, there are good reasons, given what we know about the benefits of such approaches, for investing resources into wider family and community links. This might be a particular priority where parental involvement has been neglected on the grounds that parents are 'uninterested', or where it is possible to identify parents whose willingness to become involved is not matched by their confidence and skills. In these cases, a relatively small investment might bring significant rewards.

- There are also good reasons for schools to involve themselves in a range of partnerships in what we have called (non-pejoratively) the 'peripheral' areas of their work, such as provision for vulnerable children, personal and social education and mentoring.

- Given the pressures on schools' financial and other resources, it would make sense for leadership and resourcing to be offered at local (for example, LEA, TEC, EAZ) level wherever possible. This is particularly so where multi-strand initiatives are planned. In these cases, the involvement of a number of agencies will be necessary and it will be important to develop a coherent rationale for the initiative, build consensus around that rationale and devise a management structure which is appropriately 'tight-loose'.

- Although local evaluations are limited in their wider usefulness, they are essential for internal monitoring and development purposes, given that there are no 'universal solutions' in this field. They should be built into initiatives from the start, be conducted as independently as possible and feed back regularly into the development of the project.

At national level:
- There is a need at national level for a formalisation of some of what has been learned over recent years, particularly, perhaps, in terms of parental involvement in children's learning.

The government has recently shown itself to be willing to 'package' what it regards as best practice in literacy and numeracy and, specifically, in literacy summer schools, homework clubs and the like. While such packaging runs the risk of promoting unreflective implementation, it is, handled sensitively, preferable to the current situation in which schools are left to find their own salvation.

- Similarly, there is a need for a prioritisation of school-family-community links at national level. The current emphasis on within-school provision and the patchwork of bolt-on funding arrangements inevitably means that many schools are compelled to accord such links a lower priority than might otherwise be the case. The government, however, has levers which it might pull to increase the prioritisation (and the appropriate resourcing) of school-family-community links. These include Standards Fund, LEA Education Development Plans, Behaviour Support Plans, local authority Children's Service Plans and the Ofsted frameworks for inspecting schools and LEAs, together with its range of mechanisms for directing other relevant bodies such as social services departments, TECs and health authorities. It has options which range from substantial increases in funding in this area (for instance, to fund parents' centres or community teachers) through to no-cost strategies (such as requiring schools and LEAs to develop appropriate policies within existing resources) and from 'blanket' strategies applying to all schools to targeted strategies applying, for instance, only to schools in areas experiencing multiple disadvantage. What matters most, perhaps, is the continuity and sustainability of whatever strategies are adopted so that government initiatives do not simply result in another round of short-term, bolt-on projects.

- Specifically, there are good reasons for suggesting that national government should become involved in supporting large-scale and well-researched projects which can be properly evaluated (as described above) and can contribute to the knowledge base in this field. Such projects are beyond the scope of individual schools and, even, individual LEAs in their development, their continued resourcing and their evaluation. They demand a 'programmatic' approach parallel to that proposed for research and more common, perhaps, in the USA than in the UK. Nonetheless, recent initiatives such as the first wave of New Community Schools in Scotland offer a partial model of how such large-scale projects might be constructed – though hopefully with evaluation built in from the start rather than added on afterwards.

- More fundamentally, there are tensions in overall educational and social policy which can only be resolved at national level. Throughout this review, we have seen how professional imperatives consistently override parental and community needs and how the education reforms of the past decade and more have exacerbated this phenomenon. The government is currently in the midst of a 'crusade for standards' which promises to create high quality schools and high-achieving students in all communities, but which is also requiring schools to obey clear and somewhat narrowly-focused imperatives. At the same time, the government is waging a campaign against social exclusion which implies that schools might

have a wider community role, particularly in areas experiencing multiple disadvantage. There is evidence throughout this report and elsewhere (see, for example, Clark *et al.*, 1999a, b) that many schools are likely to find it very difficult to reconcile an extension of their community role with the need to drive up standards. Insofar as they are able to square that particular circle (and there are, as we have seen, ways in which community involvement actually contributes to raised standards), it seems improbable that they will be able to heed a genuine parental and community voice if that voice is not entirely consonant with their immediate priorities.

An interviewee in one of the research projects cited in this review (Atkins, *et al.*, 1996) used a metaphor which neatly illustrates the policy options open to the government. Speaking as a community health worker, he talked of the need to 'swim upstream' from the immediate manifestations of ill-health to its sources in underlying social conditions. This metaphor allows us to suggest three 'ideal-type' roles which the government might assign to schools in attempting to reconcile its standards and social exclusion agendas. While these roles are not based on any specific aspect of the research evidence we have reviewed here, they nonetheless seem to capture the alternatives that schools actually find themselves facing and may be a useful aid to clear thinking in this complex area:

– The downstream school is concerned primarily with what we have called the 'core business' of delivering the curriculum and driving up standards of attainment within that curriculum.

Such a school can function unproblematically in areas where it can count on the unsolicited support of its parent body and where neither the community it serves nor its individual pupils bring with them major problems. In other areas, its contribution to the community is made primarily by the quality of the education it offers. However, in order to deliver that quality, it will need to be surrounded by powerful non-educational mechanisms for addressing fundamental community problems and a range of professionals (Educational Psychologists, Education Welfare Officers, School Nurses) with an extended role or entirely new kinds of 'para-educationalists' who can link school, family and community, leaving teachers free to concentrate on the curriculum.

– The midstream school is typical of many contemporary schools. While its core business remains the curriculum, it acknowledges both that effective teaching and its wider pastoral responsibilities to its pupils demand that it engage more fully with its parents and community. This it does partly through its own efforts (through the sorts of projects reported here) and partly in collaboration with other community agencies. The keys to the effectiveness of the midstream school are the extent to which it can reconcile its 'dual focus' and the quality of the collaborative networks it can establish with other agencies. The key to its overall contribution to the community is the extent to which there are mechanisms (such as currently do not exist) which allow genuine community voices to have at least some influence in determining policy and practice.

– The upstream school is of a kind which is most

closely approached in some of the more ambitious community and regeneration-oriented projects reported in the previous chapter. Instead of engaging with parents and community only where educational imperatives demand such engagement, it is a full partner in addressing wider community issues. It is thus locked into regeneration initiatives and social and economic policy at local level, operating as a resource for the community rather than simply seeing the community as a resource for itself. This in turn demands that it is highly responsive to the needs and wishes of the community (with appropriate mechanisms for community input into decision-making) and that its staff become para-community workers, seeing this extended role as part of their 'core business' rather than simply as a distraction. This also means that teachers and workers from other community agencies are likely to spend a good deal of time working in collaborative teams with common aims.

There are advantages and disadvantages in each of these three 'ideal types. More importantly, they represent fundamentally different ethical and political positions regarding the proper relationship between schools and communities. They also represent different views as to how endemic problems of social disadvantage are to be overcome – whether through an essentially individualistic strategy of raising the attainments and skill-levels of children and young people in disadvantaged localities, or through a more community-oriented approach towards regeneration. While such decisions inevitably fall in the final analysis to national governments, it is notable that the government currently is driving all schools 'downstream' while urging some schools to move simultaneously 'upstream'. No doubt a few, well-resourced schools with committed managers and creative staff will manage to stretch themselves in this way. The danger is, however, that many will choose to simplify the task by abandoning their wider community commitments and a few will simply sink without trace under the strain.

Evaluative and research literature

Adams, J. *et al.* (1994) 'She'll have a go at anything: Towards an Equal Opportunities Policy', in Abbott, L. and Rodger, R. (Eds.), *Quality in the Early Years.* Buckingham and Philadelphia: Open University Press

Ainscow, M., Farrell, P., Tweddle, D. and Malki, G. (1999) *Effective Practice in Inclusion and in Special and Mainstream Schools Working Together.* Norwich: HMSO.

ALBSU (1993) *Parents and Their Children: The Intergenerational Effects of Poor Literacy Skills.* London: ALBSU.

Alexander, T. (1997) *Family Learning: The Foundation of Effective Education.* London: Demos.

Alexander, T. *et al.* (1996) 'Learning Begins at Home: Implications for a Learning Society', in Bastiani, J. and Wolfendale, S. (Eds.), *Home-School Work in Britain, Review, Reflection and Development.* London: David Fulton.

Alexander, T. and Clyne, P. (1995) *Riches Beyond Price.* Leicester: NIACE.

Allan, J. (1992) *Providing Learning Support Through Area Teams.* Edinburgh: Scottish Council for Research in Education.

Allan, J. and Munn, P. (1992) *Teaming-Up Area Teams for Learning-Support.* Edinburgh: Scottish Council for Research in Education.

Anderson, S., Delop, G., Ettridge, M., Wetz, D. Frost, L. and Katz, I. (1995) *NSPCC Counselling in School Project Evaluation.* NSPCC.

Armstrong, D. (1995) *Power and Partnership in Education: Parents, Children and Special Educational Needs.* London: Routledge.

Armstrong, F. and Moon, B. (1993) *Rowntree Project Young People in Difficulties First Year Evaluation Report.* York: Joseph Rowntree Foundation.

Arrowsmith, J. (1990) *Improving Home-School Communication in Secondary School.* Edinburgh: Scottish Council for Research in Education.

Arrowsmith, J., Lamont, D. and Murray, J. (1992) *Sharing Action and Evaluation: Parents and Staff Working Together in Early Education.* Edinburgh: Scottish Council for Research in Education.

Atkins, M., Dyson, A. and Easen, P. (1996) *Conceptualisations of Professional Practice and Interprofessional Collaboration.* Newcastle upon Tyne: Department of Education, University of Newcastle.

Atkinson, D. (1994) *Radical Solutions, Urban Renaissance for City Schools and Communities.* London: Cassell.

Balding, J. (1992) 'Ticking the Topics: Did the School Get Them Right?' *Education and Health,* 10(3), 43–46.

Ball, M. (1998) *School Inclusion: The School, the Family and the Community.* York: Joseph Rowntree Foundation.

Ball, S.J. (1993) 'The Market as a Class Strategy in the UK and US', *British Journal of Sociology of Education,* 14(1), 3–19.

Ball, S.J., Bowe, R. and Gewirtz, S. (1996) 'Circuits

of Schooling: a Sociological Exploration of Parental Choice in Social Class Contexts', *Sociological Review*, 43, 52–78.

Barber, M. (1997) *A Reading Revolution: How We Can Teach Every Child to Read Well*, published for consultation 27 February, 1997. London: DfEE.

Barber, M. and Dann, R. (Eds.), (1996) *Raising Educational Standards in the Inner Cities, Practical Initiatives in Action*. London: Cassell.

Barber, M., Denning, T., Gough, G. and Johnson, M. (1996) 'Urban Education Initiatives: Three Case Studies', in Barber, M. and Dann, R. (Eds.) *Raising Educational Standards in the Inner Cities, Practical Initiatives in Action*. London: Cassell.

Barton, D. (1995) 'Exploring Family Literacy' *Reading*, 29(3) 2–4.

Basic Skills Agency (1998) *What Works in Secondary Schools? Catching up with Basic Skills*. London: Basic Skills Agency.

Basic Skills Agency and The Prince's Trust (1998) *Promoting Literacy Through Study Support*. London: Basic Skills Agency and Prince's Trust.

Bastiani, J. (1988) *Parents and Teachers 2, From Policy to Practice*. London: NFER-Nelson.

Bastiani, J. (1989a) 'Professional Ideology Versus Lay Experience', in Allen, G. *et al* (Eds.), *Community Education: An Agenda for Educational Reform*. Milton Keynes: Open University Press.

Bastiani, J. (1989b) *Working with Parents, a Whole School Approach*. London: NFER-Nelson.

Bastiani, J. (1991) 'Home-school Partnership. Fallacy: A Change of Teachers' Attitudes is all that is Needed', in O'Hagen, B. (Ed.), *The Charnwood Papers: Fallacies in Community Education*. Derby: Education Now.

Bastiani, J. (1995) *Taking a Few Risks, Learning from Each Other – Teachers, Parents and Pupils*. London: RSA.

Bastiani, J. (1996a) *Home-School Contracts and Agreements – Opportunity or Threat*. London: RSA.

Bastiani, J. (1996b) 'Home-School Liaison: the Mainstreaming of Good Ideas and Effective Practice', in Bastiani, J. and Wolfendale, S. (Eds.), *Home-School Work in Britain, Review, Reflection and Development*. London: David Fulton.

Bastiani, J. (1997). *Share: An Evaluation of the Pilot Programme, September 1996–1997*. Coventry: CEDC.

Bastiani, J. and Doyle, N. (1994) *Home and School: Building a Better Partnership*. London: National Consumer Council.

Bastiani, J. (1993) 'No-one ever said it was going to be easy! Some Features of the Problematic Nature of Home-School Relations in the UK', in Merttens, R. *et al.* (Eds.) *Ruling the Margins: Problematising Parental Involvement*. London: University of North London.

Baxter, J. (1998) *Final Report to DfEE on The Place To Be*. London: The Place To Be.

Bell, A. and Sigsworth, A. (1992) *The Heart of the*

Community: Rural Primary Schools and Community Development. Norwich: Mousehold Press.

Bell, G., Barry, S., Fletcher, J. and Naish, L. (1997) 'School Watch: Working with Pupils to make Schools Safer Places', in Tattum, D. and Herbert, G. (Eds.), *Bullying, Home, School and Community*. London: David Fulton.

Bellaby, P. (1977) *The Sociology of Comprehensive Schooling*. London: Methuen.

Bentley, T. (1998) *Learning Beyond the Classroom: Education for a Changing World*. London and New York: Routledge.

Beresford, E. (1992) 'The Politics of Parental Involvement', in Allen, G. and Martin, I. (Eds.), *Education and Community. The Politics of Practice*. London: Cassell.

Beresford, E. and Hardie, A. (1996) 'Parents and Secondary Schools: A Different Approach', in Bastiani, J. and Wolfendale, S. (Eds.), *Home-School Work in Britain, Review, Reflection and Development*. London: David Fulton.

Bernstein, B. (1970) 'Education Cannot Compensate for Society'. *New Society*, 26, 344–347.

Beverton, S. (1995) 'Whose Literacy? School, Community or Family?' *Reading*, 29(3), 14–18.

Birchfield Community Primary School (1998) 'Working with Parents and the Community to Raise Achievement at Birchfield', in DIECEC (Ed.), *Pathways to Intercultural Education and Raising Achievement*. Bradford: DIECEC.

Black, H., Malcolm, H. and Bankowska, A.(1992) *Furthering Education? Links Between Schools and Further Education Colleges in Lothian Region* (41). Edinburgh: Scottish Council for Research in Education.

Blair, A., McPake, J and Munn, P. (1995) *Having Adults Studying in your School*. Edinburgh: Scottish Council for Research in Education.

Blandford, S. (1998) *Managing Discipline in Schools*. London: Routledge.

Body, W. (1990) *Helping Your Child with Reading*. London: BBC Books.

Border, R. and Merttens, R. (1993) 'Parental Partnership: Comfort or Conflict.' In Merttens, R. and Vass, J. (Eds.), *Partnerships in Maths: Parents and Schools: The IMPACT Project*. London: Falmer Press.

Borland, L. (1991) 'Link Courses, Using Settings Outside School', in Hustler, D. *et al.* (Eds.), *Learning Environments for the Whole Curriculum*. London: Hyman.

Bottery, M. (1993) 'The Management of Schools and Citizenship'. *Citizenship*, 3(1), 6–7.

Bowen, S. and Bennett, R. (1998) *Education Business Partnership Survey: Report of Key Findings, Business Growth Project*. Cambridge: Department of Geography, University of Cambridge.

Branston, P. (1996) 'Children and Parents Enjoying Reading', in Wolfendale, S. and Topping, K. (Eds.) *Family Involvement in Literacy*. London: Cassell.

Brehony, K. (1995) 'School Governors: "Race" and

"Racism"', in Tomlinson, S. and Craft, M. (Eds.), *Ethnic Relations and Schooling: Policy and Practice in the 1990s*. London: Athlone.

Bridge, M. (1998) *Eastfield Open Doors Project 1997–1998*. Scarborough: Yorkshire Coast College, Braeburn Infant and Nursery School.

Bridgwood, A. (1996) 'Consortium Collaboration: The Experience of TVEI', in Bridges, D. and Husbands, C. (Eds.), *Consorting and Collaborating in the Education Marketplace*. London: Falmer Press.

Brighouse, T. (1991) 'Fallacy: A National Curriculum is Incompatible with a Community Curriculum', in O'Hagen, B. (Ed.), *The Charnwood Papers: Fallacies in Community Education*. Derby: Education Now.

Brighouse, T. (1993) 'Parents' Expectations of Primary Schools', in Merttens, R. *et al.* (Eds.), *Ruling the Margins: Problematising Parental Involvement*. London: University of North London.

Bristow, D. (1993) 'IMPACT in the Urban Authority', in Merttens, R. and Vass, J. (Eds.), *Partnerships in Maths: Parents and Schools: The IMPACT Project*. London: Falmer Press.

Britto, J. and Waller, H. (1993) 'Partnership – At What Price?', in Merttens, R. *et al.* (Eds.), *Ruling the Margins: Problematising Parental Involvement*. London: University of North London.

Brooks, G., Gorman, T., Harman, J., Hutchinson, D. and Wilkin, A. (1996) *Family Literacy Works*. London: Basic Skills Agency.

Brown, A. (1993) 'Participation Dialogue and the Reproduction of Social Inequalities', in Merttens, R. and Vass, J. (Eds.), *Partnerships in Maths: Parents and Schools: The IMPACT Project*. London: Falmer Press.

Brown, P. (1997) 'The Third Wave: Education and the Ideology of Parentocracy', in Halsey, A.H. *et al.*(Eds.), *Education, Culture, Economy and Society*. Oxford and New York: Oxford University Press.

Bryans, T. (1989) 'Parental Involvement in Primary Schools: Contemporary Issues', in Wolfendale, S. (Ed.), *Parental Involvement: Developing Networks between School, Home and Community*. London: Cassell.

Bryce, A. (1999) *Improving School Attendance Project, Strategic Development and Summary Report*. Lancashire Education Authority.

Cairney, T. H. (1996) 'Developing Partnerships with Families in Literacy and Learning', in Wolfendale, S. and Topping, K. (Eds.), *Family Involvement in Literacy*. London: Cassell.

Calderdale and Kirklees TEC (1998) *A Development Project involving Parents in their Children's Education – Evaluation Report September 1996 – April 1998*. Calderdale and Kirklees TEC.

Calliste, J. (1993) 'Partnership with Parents: A Model for Practice', *Educational Psychology in Practice*, 9(2), 73–81.

Calvert, L. (1993) 'IMPACT Does it Really Make a Difference? A Teacher's Personal View', in Merttens, R. and Vass, J. (Eds.), *Partnerships in Maths: Parents and Schools: The IMPACT Project*. London: Falmer Press.

Capper, L., Downes, P. and Jenkinson, D. (1998) *Successful Schools, Parental Involvement in Secondary Schools*. Coventry: CEDC.

Carrie, K. (1993) 'A Probationer's Year on IMPACT's Probationary Year', in Merttens, R. and Vass, J. (Eds.), *Partnerships in Maths: Parents and Schools: The IMPACT Project*. London: Falmer Press.

Carspecken, P. F. (1991) *Community Schooling and the Nature of Power: The Battle for Croxteth Comprehensive*. London: Routledge.

CEDC (1997) *Consultant's Report on Partnership Project in Nottinghamshire*. Coventry: Community Education Development Centre.

Centre for Educational Research and Innovation (1997) *Parents as Partners in Schooling*. Paris: OECD.

Chaplain, R. and Gray, S. (1999) *Education Business Partnerships: Understanding the Students' Contribution. First Report on a Project commissioned by the National EBP Network*. Cambridge: Homerton College, University of Cambridge.

Chapman, C. (1996) 'Empowering Pupils through Home-School Links', in Bastiani, J. and Wolfendale, S. (Eds.), *Home-School Work in Britain, Review, Reflection and Development*. London: David Fulton.

Chapman, D. and Aspin, N. (1997) *The School, the Community and Lifelong Learning*. London: Cassell.

Clancy, K., Dunne, C. and Macbeth, A. (1998)

Education is Much More than Schooling, Study Materials on Home, School and Community. Glasgow: St Andrews College.

Clark, C., Dyson, A., Millward, A. and Robson, S. (1999a) 'Inclusive Education and Schools as Organisations', *International Journal of Inclusive Education*, 3(1), 37–51.

Clark, C., Dyson, A., Millward, A. and Robson, S. (1999b) 'Theories of Inclusion, Theories of Schools: Deconstructing and Reconstructing the "Inclusive School"', *British Educational Research Journal*, 25(2), 157–177.

Clark, D. (1992) 'Education for Community in the 1990s: A Christian Perspective', in Allen, G. and Martin, I. (Eds.), *Education and Community. The Politics of Practice*. London: Cassell.

Clark, D. (1996) *Schools as Learning Communities: Transforming Education*. London: Cassell.

Cockett, M. (1991) 'Assessing Learning', in Hustler, D. *et al.*(Eds.), *Learning Environments for the Whole Curriculum*. London: Hyman.

Cook, P. and Dalton, R. (1989) 'Schools and Communities: The Hertfordshire 2000 Project', in Sayer, J. and Williams, V. (Eds.), *Schools and External Relations, Managing the New Partnerships*. London: Cassell.

Copland, D. (1998) *Lessons in Class: A Fresh Appraisal of Comprehensive Education*. Newcastle upon Tyne: TUPS Books.

Crime Concern (1998a) *Partners for Life: Young People*

and Community Safety. Swindon: Pru Youth Action, Crime Concern.

Crime Concern (1998b) *Partners for Life: Young People and Community Safety: Taking Action on Bullying.* Swindon: Pru Youth Action, Crime Concern.

Crime Concern (1998c) *Partners in Community Safety, Crime Concern and Training Services.* Swindon: Pru Youth Action, Crime Concern.

Croydon, E.B.P. (1997). *Primary School Mentoring Scheme: Evaluation Report.* Croydon: Croydon EBP.

Crozier, G. (1996) 'Black Parents and School Relationships: A Case Study', *Educational Review,* 48(3), 253–267.

Crozier, G. (1998) *Is it a Case of 'We Know When We're Not Wanted?' The Parents' Perspective on Parent-Teacher Roles and Relationships.* Paper presented at the British Educational Research Association Annual Conference.

Cuckle, P. (1996) 'Children Learning to Read – Exploring Home and School relationships', *British Educational Research Journal,* 22(1), 17–32.

Curle, D. (1993) 'IMPACT and Cultural Diversity', in Merttens, R. and Vass, J. (Eds.), *Partnerships in Maths: Parents and Schools: The IMPACT Project.* London: Falmer Press.

Daly, L. (1999) *Evaluation of Information and Support Provided by Coventry Education Service for Parents/Carers of Children with Special Educational Needs in Coventry.* Coventry: City of Coventry Education Service.

Darling, S. (1993) 'Family Literacy: An Intergenerational Approach to Literature', *Viewpoints.* Basic Skills Agency, 2-5.

Dasgupta, C. and Richards, M. (1997) 'Support for Children of Separating Parents', *Developing Practice in Representing Children,* 10(2), 106–116.

David, M., Edwards, R., Hughes, M. and Ribbens, J. (1993) *Mothers and Education: Inside Out. Exploring Family Education Policy and Experience.* London: Macmillan.

David, M.E. (1993) *Parents, Gender and Education Reform.* Cambridge: Polity Press.

Davies, L. (1999) *School Councils and Pupil Exclusions.* London: School Councils UK

Davis, C. and Stubb, R. (1988) *Shared Reading in Practice.* Milton Keynes: Open University Press.

Davis, J. (1989) 'Liverpool's Parent Support Programme: A Case Study', in Allen, G. *et al* (Eds.), *Community Education: An Agenda for Educational Reform.* Milton Keynes: Open University Press.

Day, G. and Kannike, Y. (1999) *Roots and Wings Mentoring Project: Monitoring Report 1998/1999.* London: The Roots and Wings Mentoring Scheme.

Deem, R., Brehony, R. and Heath, S. (1995) *Active Citizenship and the Governing of Schools.* Buckingham: Open University Press.

Deloughty, F. (1991) 'Nursery Placements, Using Settings Outside School', in Hustler, D. *et al.* (Eds.),

Learning Environments for the Whole Curriculum. London: Hyman.

Dench, S. and O'Regan, S. (1998) *Helping Parents to Work: A Study for Kent TEC.* Brighton: The Institute for Employment Studies.

Derby City Council (1997) *Report of the Derby Family Literacy Project (SRB) 1996–97.* Derby: Derby City Council.

Derby City Council (1998). *Report of the Derby Family Literacy Project (SRB) 1997–98.* Derby: Derby City Council.

DES (1991) *A Sporting Double: School and Community.* London: HMSO.

DETR (1997) *Education Initiatives and Regeneration Strategies. A Guide to Good Practice.* London: Department of Environment, Transport and the Regions.

Devine, M. (1993) *Supporting Health Education in Schools.* Edinburgh: Scottish Council for Research in Education.

Devine, M. (1996) *Working With Others in School Health Education Programmes.* Edinburgh: Scottish Council for Research in Education.

DfEE (1996) *Equipping Young People for Working Life. A Consultative Document on Improving Employability Through the 14–16 Curriculum.* London: DfEE.

DfEE (1997a) 'Engaging Parents, Dorset LEA', in *Innovation in Drug Education.* London: DfEE.

DfEE (1997b) 'Involving Local Sports, Bradford LEA', in *Innovation in Drug Education.* London: DfEE.

DfEE (1997c) 'A Multi-Agency Approach "500 for Health" Devon LEA', in *Innovation in Drug Education.* London: DfEE.

DfEE (1997d) 'Parents' Awareness Programme, Cambridgeshire LEA', in *Innovation in Drug Education.* London: DfEE.

DfEE (1997e) 'Theatre in Education, Brent LEA', in *Innovation in Drug Education.* London: DfEE.

DfEE (1998a) *Extending Opportunity: A National Framework for Study Support.* London: DfEE.

DfEE (1998b) *Numeracy Matters: The Preliminary Report of the Numeracy Task Force.* London: DfEE.

DfEE (1998c) *Specialist Schools: Education Partnerships for the 21st Century (SPBG007).* London: DfEE.

DfEE (1999) *Excellence in Cities.* London: DfEE.

DIECEC (1998) *Pathways to Intercultural Education and Raising Achievement.* Bradford: DIECEC.

Dimmock, C.A.J. and Donoghue, T.A. (1996) 'Parental Involvement in Schooling: An Emerging Research Agenda', *Compare*, 26(1), 5–20.

Docking, J. (1990) *Primary Schools and Parents, Rights, Responsibilities and Relationships.* London: Hodder and Stoughton.

Douglas, J.W.B. (1964) *The Home and the School.* London: MacGibbon and Kee.

Drysdale, G. (1998) *The School-Home Liaison Project Annual Report 1997–1998.* London: The London Diocesan Board for Schools.

Duncan, C. (1989) 'Home, School and Community in a Multiracial Context', in Wolfendale, S. (Ed.), *Parental Involvement: Developing Networks Between School, Home and Community.* London: Cassell.

Dyson, A. (1997) 'Social and Educational Disadvantage: Reconnecting Special Needs Education', *British Journal of Special Education,* 24(4), 152–157.

Dyson, A. (1998) 'Professional Intellectuals from Powerful Groups: Wrong from the Start', in Clough, P. and Barton, L. (Eds.), *Articulating with Difficulty: Research Voices in Inclusive Education.* London: Paul Chapman Publications.

Dyson, A., Lin, M. and Millward, A. (1998) *Effective Communications Between Schools, LEAs and Health Services in the Field of Special Educational Needs* (60). London: DfEE.

Easen, P., Ford, K., Higgins, S., Todd, L. and Wootten, M. (1996) *The Educational Achievement Strategy.* Newcastle upon Tyne: University of Newcastle.

Easen, P., Kendall, P. and Shaw, J. (1992) 'Parents and Educators: Dialogue and Development through Partnership', *Children and Society,* 6(4), 282–296.

Education Extra (1997a) *Succeeding Out of School, Out of School Childcare Initiative.* London: DfEE.

Education Extra (1997b) *Summer Literacy Schemes in Wales, The Education Extra Evaluation.* Welsh Office and Education Extra.

Education Extra (1997c) *The Summer Literacy Schools, An Evaluation of the 1997 Pilot Scheme.* London: DfEE.

Edwards, A. and Knight, P. (1994) *Effective Early Years Education.* Buckingham: Open University Press.

Edwards, R. and David, M. (1997) 'Where are all the Children in Home-School Relations? Notes towards a Research Agenda', *Children and Society,* 11, 194–200.

Edwards, S., Chauhan, S. and Skoulding, H. (1997) *Innovative Therapeutic Groupwork in Schools, Project Evaluation Report.* Northampton: St George's Middle School.

Elliott, J.A. (1998a) *An Evaluation of the Family Literacy Project.* Hartlepool: Hartlepool LEA.

Elliott, J.A. (1998b) *An Evaluation of the Helping in Schools Project.* Hartlepool: Hartlepool LEA.

Evans, D. (1998) *Report on the Evaluation of the Family Literacy Initiative.* Essex LEA Adult Education Service.

Family Nurturing Network (1999) *Programmes Evaluation Report.* Oxford: The Family Nurturing Network.

Fielding, M. (1996) 'Beyond Collaboration: On the Importance of Community', in Bridges, D. and Husbands, C. (Eds.), *Consorting and Collaborating in the Education Marketplace.* London: Falmer Press.

Fitzherbert, K. and Yeo, S. (1997) 'Using Group

Dynamics to Support Vulnerable Children: Including Victims of School Bullying', in Tattum, D. and Herbert, G. (Eds.), *Bullying, Home, School and Community*. Lincoln: David Fulton.

Fletcher, C. (1991) 'A Policy is Everything or Nothing', In O'Hagan, B. (Ed.), *The Charnwood Papers: Fallacies in Community Education*. Derby: Education Now.

Fletcher, C. and Bramley, G. (1996) *Evaluating Quality in Community Education within a Regional Context*. Paper Presented at ECER96 Seville.

Floud, J. (1961) 'Social Class Factors in Educational Achievement', in Halsey, A.H. (Ed.), *Ability and Educational Opportunity*. Paris: OECD.

Floud, J.E., Halsey, A.H. and Martin, F.M. (1956) *Social Class and Educational Opportunity*. London: Heinemann.

Fowler, W.S. (1989) *Teachers, Parents and Governors*. London: Kogan Page.

Fraser, H. (1998) *Early Intervention: Key Issues from Research (Interchange 50)*. Moray House Institute of Education.

Frater, G. (1997) *Improving Boys' Literacy: A Survey of Effective Practice in Secondary Schools*. London: Basic Skills Agency.

Gale, S. (1996) 'Setting up a Parents' Advice Centre: Partnership or PR?', in Bastiani, J. and Wolfendale, S. (Eds.), *Home-School Work in Britain, Review, Reflection and Development*. London: David Fulton.

Gale, S. and Hancock, R. (1996) 'Hackney PACT: Reflecting on the Experience of Promoting Home Reading Schemes', in S. Wolfendale and K. Topping (Eds.), *Family Involvement in Literacy*. London: Cassell.

Gallacher, N. (1995) 'Partnership in Education', in Macbeth, A. *et al.* (Eds.), *Collaborate or Compete? Educational Partnerships in a Market Economy*. London: Falmer Press.

Gardner, A. and Semple, S. (1995) *Getting the Message Across: Education Industry Links in Scotland*. Edinburgh: Scottish Council for Research in Education.

Gascoigne, E. (1995) *Working with Parents as Partners in SEN*. London: David Fulton.

Gatenby, R. (1998) *Out of School Childcare Initiative: An Evaluation of Long-Term Sustainability (RR48)*. London: DfEE.

George, R. (1998) *Reducing School Exclusions: What Works? A Review of Good Practice in the Thames Valley*. Thame: Thames Valley Partnership.

Gerwitz, S., Ball, S.J. and Bowe, R. (1995) *Markets, Choice and Equity in Education*. Buckingham: Open University Press.

Giles, R. (1992) 'Defending Community Education in Schools: An LEA Strategy', in Allan, G. and Martin, I. (Eds.), *Education and Community. The Politics of Practice*. London: Cassell.

Gill, K. and Pickles, T. (Eds.) (1989) *Active Collaboration, Joint Practice and Youth Strategies*. Glasgow: ITRC.

Gledhill, J. (1995) *Engaging Communities*. Bradford: City of Bradford Metropolitan Borough Council, Directorate of Housing and Environmental Protection.

Glynn, T. (1996) 'Pause, Prompt Praise: Reading Tutoring Procedures for Home and School Partnership', in Wolfendale, S. and Topping, K. (Eds.), *Family Involvement in Literacy*. London: Cassell.

Golby, M., Brigley, S., Lane, B., Taylor, W. and Viant, R. (1989) *The New Governors Speak*. Tiverton: Fair Way Publications.

Golden, S. and Sims, D. (1997) *Evaluation of the Delivery of NVQs/SVQs in Further Education* (Research Studies No. RS45). London: DfEE.

Graham, J. (1998) *What Works in Reducing Criminality*. London: Home Office, Research and Statistics Directorate.

Greenhough, P. and Hughes, M. (1998) 'Parents' and Teachers' Interventions in Children's Reading', *British Educational Research Journal*, 24(4), 383–398.

Gregory, E. (1996) 'Learning from the Community: A Family Literacy Project with Bangladeshi Children in London', in Wolfendale, S. and Topping, K. (Eds.), *Family Involvement in Literacy*. London: Cassell.

Gregory, E. (Ed.) (1997) *One Child, Many Worlds. Early Learning in Multicultural Communities*. London: David Fulton.

Grimshaw, R. and McGurie, C. (1998) *Evaluating Parenting Programmes: A Study of Stakeholders' Views (Research Summary)*. London: National Children's Bureau.

Guishard, J. (1998) 'The Parents' Support Service: Brief Family Work in a School Context', *Educational Psychology in Practice*, 14(2), 135–139.

Hall, S., Kay, I. and Struthers, S. (1992) *The Experience of Partnership in Education: Parents, Professionals and Children*. Dereham: Peter Francis Publishers.

Halsey, A.H. (Ed.). (1972) *Educational Priority: EPA Problems and Practices*. London: HMSO.

Hancock, R. (1998) 'Building Home-School Liaison into Classroom Practice: A Need to Understand the Nature of a Teacher's Working Day', *British Educational Research Journal*, 24(4), 399–414.

Hancock, R., O'Connor, A., Jenner, H., Ostmo, G. and Sheath, G. (1996) 'Making School More Visible to Parents: An Evaluation of the Harbinger Video Project', in Bastiani, J. and Wolfendale, S. (Eds.), *Home-School Work in Britain, Review, Reflection and Development*. London: David Fulton.

Hand, J. (1995) *Raising Standards in Schools: The Youth Work Contribution*. Leicester: Youth Work Press.

Hand, J. and Wright, W. (1997) *Youth Work in Colleges, Building on Partnership*. London: FEDA.

Hannon, P. (1992) 'Intergenerational Literacy Intervention: Possibilities and Problems', *Viewpoints*. Basic Skills Agency, 6–8.

Hannon, P. (1993) 'Conditions of Learning at Home

and in School', in Merttens, R. *et al.* (Eds.) *Ruling the Margins: Problematising Parental Involvement.* London: University of North London.

Hannon, P. (1995) *Literacy, Home and School: Research and Practice in Teaching Literacy with Parents.* London: Falmer Press.

Hannon, P. (1996) 'Pre-school work with Parents', in Wolfendale, S. and Topping, K. (Eds.), *Family Involvement in Literacy.* London: Cassell.

Hannon, P. and Nutbrown, C. (1998) *First Year Project Report to Nuffield Foundation. A Longitudinal Study of Pre-school Home Focused Literacy Education.* Sheffield: University of Sheffield.

Hannon, P. and Nutbrown, C.J. (1997) 'Taking Parent Learning Seriously,' *Adult Learning* (Nov. 1997), 19–21.

Harding, J. (1988) 'Parental Involvement: Developing a Partnership and a Policy', *Management in Education*, 2(4), 38–41.

Hartley, D. (1994) 'Mixed Messages in Education Policy: Sign of the Times?', *British Journal of Educational Studies*, 42(3), 230–244.

Hawes, H. and Stephens, D. (1990) *Questions of Quality: Primary Education and Development.* London: Longman.

Hayden, C. (1997) *Children Excluded from Primary School: Debates, Evidence, Responses.* Buckingham: OUP.

Hemstedt, A. (1995) 'A Good Start for Learning:

Family Literacy Work by the Basic Skills Agency', *Reading*, 29(3) 10–14.

Hendry, L., Shucksmith, J. and Philip, K. (1995) *Educating for Health.* London: Cassell.

Hewison, J. (1988) 'The Long-term Effectiveness of Parental Involvement in Reading: a follow-up to the Haringey Reading Project', *British Journal of Educational Psychology* (58), 184–190.

Hewison, J. and Tizard, J. (1980) 'Parental Involvement and Reading Attainment', *British Journal of Educational Psychology*(50), 209–215.

Hillage, J. (1995) *Employers' Views of Education Business Links* (283). Grantham: Institute for Employment Studies.

Hinton, S. (1989) 'Dimensions of Parental Involvement: Easing the Transfer from Pre-school to Primary,' in Wolfendale, S. (Ed.), *Parental Involvement: Developing Networks between School, Home and Community.* London: Cassell.

Hira, S. and Masson, S. (1998) 'Supplementary Schools and Learning of Community Languages in Birmingham', in DIECEC (Ed.), *Pathways to Intercultural Education and Raising Achievement.* Bradford: DIECEC.

Hirst, K. (1998) 'Pre-school Literacy Experiences of Children in Punjabi, Urdu and Gujarati Speaking Families in England', *British Educational Research Journal*, 24(4), 415–429.

Hitchcock, G. (1988) *Education and Training 14–18: A Survey of Major Initiatives.* London: Longman.

HMI (1990) *A Survey of School Based Youth and Community Work* (244/91/ns). Her Majesty's Inspectorate.

Hope, P. and Sharland, P. (1997) *Tomorrow's Parents: Developing Parenthood Education in Schools*. London: Calouste Gulbenkian Foundation.

Hornby, G. (1995) *Working with Parents of Children with Special Needs*. London and New York: Cassell.

Houston, A. (1996) 'Home-School Projects: Influencing Long-term Change', in Bastiani, J. and Wolfendale, S. (Eds.), *Home-School Work in Britain, Review, Reflection and Development*. London: David Fulton.

Howard, L. (1991) 'The Community Form Project, Using Settings Outside School', in Hustler, D. *et al.*(Eds.), *Learning Environments for the Whole Curriculum*. London: Hyman.

Howarth, S. (1998) 'Enabling Parents to Support Their Children's Education in Basic Skills', in DIECEC (Ed.), *Pathways to Intercultural Education and Raising Achievement*. Bradford: DIECEC.

Howarth, S. and Fisher, L. (1998) 'Literacy in Bradford: The Better Reading Partnership', in DIECEC (Ed.), *Pathways to Intercultural Education and Raising Achievement*. Bradford: DIECEC.

Howarth, S., Rashid, J. and Ahmed, I. (1998) 'Supplementary Schools and Learning of Community Languages in Bradford', in DIECEC (Ed.), *Pathways to Intercultural Education and Raising Achievement*. Bradford: DIECEC.

Howe, D. and Wilson, J. (1995) *Bringing Learning to Life, Involving the Community in the National Curriculum*. Coventry: CEDC.

Howieson, C. and Semple, S. (1996) *Guidance in Secondary Schools*. Edinburgh: The Scottish Council for Research in Education.

Hughes, M. (1993) 'Parent's Views – Rhetoric and Reality', in Merttens, R. *et al.* (Eds.), *Ruling the Margins: Problematising Parental Involvement*. London: University of North London.

Hughes, M., Wikeley, F. and Nash, T. (1993) 'Parents in the New Era: Myth and Reality', in Merttens, R. and Vass, J. (Eds.), *Partnerships in Maths: Parents and Schools: The IMPACT Project*. London: Falmer Press.

Hughes, M., Wikeley, F. and Nash, T. (1994) *Parents and their Children's Schools*. Oxford: Blackwell.

Hunt, K. and Robson, M. (1998) 'When I'm 100, Will I Reach the Sky? The Value of Parental Involvement in Early Years Education', *Early Education*, Summer 1998, 8–9.

Hunter, S. (1993) 'Maths in my Home', in Merttens, R. and Vass, J. (Eds.), *Partnerships in Maths: Parents and Schools: The IMPACT Project*. London: Falmer Press.

Hurry, J. and Lloyd, C. (1997) *A Follow Up Evaluation of Project Charlie*. London: Home Office, Central Drugs Prevention Unit.

Husbands, C. (1996) 'Schools, Markets and

Collaboration: New Models For Educational Policy', in Bridges, D. and Husbands, C. (Eds.), *Consorting and Collaborating in the Education Marketplace*. London: Falmer Press.

Husen, T. (1979) *The School in Question: A Comparative Study of the School and its Future in Western Societies*. Oxford: Oxford University Press

Hutchinson, J. and Campbell, M. (1999) *Working in Partnership: Lessons from the Literature* (63). London: DfEE.

Irving, B.A. and Parker-Jenkins, M. (1995) 'Tackling Truancy: An Examination of Persistent Non-attendance Amongst Disaffected School Pupils and Positive Support Strategies, *Cambridge Journal of Education*, 25(2), 225–235.

Jackson, D. and Fendall, J. (1998) 'The Interfaith Education Centre', in DIECEC (Ed.), *Pathways to Intercultural Education and Raising Achievement*. Bradford: DIECEC.

Jamison, J. (1998) *The Health Promoting School: Final Report of the ENHPS Evaluation Project in England*. London: Health Education Authority.

Jeavons, M. (1995) *Too Good to be True. An Evaluative Case Study of a Youth Initiative in a Secondary School which Successfully tackled the Issue of Crime Prevention*. Walsall: School of Education, University of Wolverhampton.

Jeffs, T. (1989) 'Youth and Community Work and the Community School', in Allen, G. and Martin, I (Eds.), *Community Education: An Agenda for Educational Reform*. Milton Keynes: Open University Press.

Jeffs, T. (1992) 'The State, Ideology and the Community School Movement', in Allen, G. and Martin, I (Eds.), *Education and Community. The Politics of Practice*. London: Cassell.

Jeffs, T. and Smith, M. (1991) 'Fallacy: The School is a Poor Base for Youth Work', in O'Hagan, B. (Ed.), *The Charnwood Papers: Fallacies in Community Education*. Derby: Education Now.

Jeffs, T. and Smith, M. (1998) 'Youth Work and Schooling', in Jeffs, T. (Ed.), *Welfare and Youth Work Practice*. Basingstoke: Macmillan.

Johnson, D. (1988) *Schools' External Relations*. Milton Keynes: Open University Press.

Johnson, M. and Barber, M. (1996) 'Collaboration for School Improvement: The Power of Partnership', in Bridges, D. and Husbands, C. (Eds.), *Consorting and Collaborating in the Education Marketplace*. London: Falmer Press.

Johnston, J. (1996) *Parents Facilitating Educational Development in the Primary Child: Current Practice and Future Development*. Paper presented at the B.E.R.A. Conference 1996.

Jones, M, and Rowley, G. (1990) 'What does Research Say about Parental Participation in Children's Reading Development, *Evaluation and Research in Education*, 4(1), 21–36.

Jowett, S., Baginsky, M. and Macdonald-McNeil, M. (1991) *Building Bridges: Parental Involvement in Schools*. Windsor: NFER-Nelson.

Kahn, T., and Sugden, C. (Eds.) (1995). *Today's*

Child, Tomorrow's Adult: Approaches to Developing Family Relationships and Effective Parenting. Coventry: CEDC.

Kemp, M. (1996) 'Parents, Teachers, Children: A Whole Literacy Education System', in Wolfendale, S. and Topping, K. (Eds.), *Family Involvement in Literacy.* London: Cassell.

Kinder, K., Kendall, S., Halsey, K. and Atkinson, M. (1999) *Disaffection Talks: A Report for the Merseyside Learning Partnership Inter Agency Development Programme.* Slough: NFER.

Kinder, K. and Wilkin, A. (1998) *With All Respect: Reviewing Disaffection Strategies.* Slough: NFER.

Kingston-upon-Hull (1999). *Adult Community Education Services: Parenting Matters.* Kingston upon Hull: Kingston upon Hull City Council.

Kirkland, J. (1991) 'The Residential, Using Settings outside School', in Hustler, D. *et al.*(Eds.), *Learning Environments for the Whole Curriculum.* London: Hyman.

Kushner, S. (1991) *The Children's Music Book: Performing Musicians in Schools.* London: Calouste Gulbenkian Foundation.

Lareau, A. (1997) 'Social Class Differences in Family-School Relationships. The Importance of Cultural Capital', in Halsey, A.H. *et al.*(Eds.), *Education, Culture, Economy and Society.* Oxford and New York: Oxford University Press.

Leming, E.P. (1997) *Summary of Suffolk LEA Report on Research into the use of Named Person by Parents of Children with SEN.* Ipswich: Suffolk County Council.

Leming, E.P. (1998) *SEN Tribunal Research Summary Report.* Ipswich: Suffolk LEA.

Leming, E.P. (1999) *Information from Parents' Focus Group.* Ipswich: Suffolk LEA.

Lindsay, G., Lloyd-Smith, M. and Crozier, J. (1998) *Lancashire Pupil Support Project, Second Interim Report.* Lancashire County Council.

Liverpool Parent School Partnership. (1996) 'The PSP Experience in Liverpool: Towards a City-wide Service', in Bastiani, J. and Wolfendale, S. (Eds.), *Home-School Work in Britain, Review, Reflection and Development.* London: David Fulton.

Lloyd, C. (1994) *The Welfare Network: How Well Does the Net Work? Young People in Difficulties – An Inter-agency Project in Oxford City.* Oxford: Oxford Brookes University.

Long, R. (1993) 'Parental Involvement or Parental Compliance? Parents and School Improvement', in Merttens, R. *et al.* (Eds.), *Ruling the Margins: Problematising Parental Involvement.* London: University of North London.

Lovett, T. (1991) 'Fallacy: Community Development Work is Subversive', in O'Hagan, B. (Ed.), *The Charnwood Papers: Fallacies in Community Education.* Derby: Education Now.

Lowden, K. and Powney, J. (1994) *Drugs, Alcohol and Sex Education, A Report Based on Two Innovative School-based Programmes (59).* Edinburgh: Scottish Council for Research in Education.

Lowden, K., and Powney, J. (1995) *Professional Partnerships in Health Education Teaching in Schools.* Edinburgh: Scottish Council for Research in Education.

Lowden, K. and Powney, J. (1996) *An Evolving Sexual Health Education Programme, From Health Workers to Teachers* (80). Edinburgh: Scottish Council for Research in Education.

Lunt, I., Evans, J., Norwich, B. and Wedell, K. (1994) *Working together – Inter-school Collaboration for Special Needs.* London: David Fulton.

Luton Education Department (1998) *Family Numeracy Report.* Luton: Luton Education Department.

Lyle, S., Benyon, J., Garland, J. and McClure, A. (1996) *Education Matters – African Caribbean People and Schools in Leicestershire.* Scarman Centre.

Macbeath, J. (1995) 'Clients Evaluating the School', in Macbeth, A. *et al.* (Eds.), *Collaborate or Compete? Educational Partnerships in a Market Economy.* London: Falmer Press.

Macbeath, J. (1996) 'Improving Schools: A home-school Partnership in Scotland, *International Journal of Education Research,* 25(1).

Macbeath, J. (1997a) *After William – Reporting to Parents.* Edinburgh: Scottish Council for Research in Education.

Macbeath, J. (1997b) *Study Support, Learning to Achieve.* London: The Prince's Trust.

Macbeth, A. (1993) 'How can Home-Learning

Become Part of our Education System?' in Merttens, R. *et al.* (Eds.), *Ruling the Margins: Problematising Parental Involvement.* London: University of North London.

Macbeth, A. (1995) 'Partnership between Parents and Teachers in Education', in Macbeth, A. *et al.* (Eds.), *Collaborate or Compete? Educational Partnerships in a Market Economy.* London: Falmer Press.

Macbeth, A. (1998) *Involving Parents: Effective Parent Teacher Relations.* Oxford: Heinemann Educational.

Mackenzie, J. (1997) *It's a Man's job. Class and Gender in School Work-Experience.* Edinburgh: Scottish Council for Research in Education.

Maclachlan, K. (1996) 'Good Mothers are Women Too: the Gender Implications of Parental Involvement in Education', in Bastiani, J. and Wolfendale, S. (Eds.), *Home-School Work in Britain, Review, Reflection and Development.* London: David Fulton.

Macleod, F. (Ed.). (1989) *Parents and Schools: the Contemporary Challenge.* London: Falmer Press.

Macleod, F.J. (1996). 'Does British Research Support Claims about the Benefits of Parents Hearing Their Children Read At Home? A Closer Look at Evidence from Three Key Studies', *Research Papers in Education,* 11(2), 173–199.

Malek, M. (1996) *Making Home-School Work: Home-School Work and the East London Schools Fund (Research Summary).* London: National Children's Bureau.

Marsh, C. (1994) 'People Matter: the role of adults

in providing a Quality Learning Environment for the early years', in Abbott, L. and Rodger, R. (Eds.), *Quality in the Early Years*. Buckingham and Philadelphia: Open University Press.

Martin, J., Ranson, S., McKeown, P. and Nixon, J. (1996) 'School Governance for the Civil Society: Redefining the Boundary Between Schools and Parents. *Local Government Studies*, 22(4), 210–228.

Masson, S. and Farror, M. (1998) 'Birmingham's University of the First Age', in DIECEC (Ed.), *Pathways to Intercultural Education and Raising Achievement*. Bradford: DIECEC.

Mayall, B. (1990) *The Parent Organiser Project at Westminster City School*. London: Gulbenkian Foundation.

McCreath, D. and Maclachlan, K. (1995) 'Realizing the Virtual New Alliances in the Market Model Education Game', in Macbeth, A. *et al.* (Eds.), *Collaborate or Compete? Educational Partnerships in a Market Economy*. London: Falmer Press.

McGurk, H. and Hurry, J. (1995) *Project Charlie: An Evaluation of a Life Skills Drug Education Programme for Primary Schools*. London: Home Office.

McNamara, D. *et al.* (1992) *Home School Liaison in Humberside – Teachers' Practices and Professional Expertise*. Hull: University of Hull.

Meldrum, B. (1998a) *Final Report on the Work of the Senior Educational Psychologist: The Place To Be*. London: The Place To Be.

Meldrum, B. (1998b) *The Place to Be Project Report*

prepared for the Board of Trustees. London: The Place To Be.

Merttens, R. (1993) 'IMPACT: Pride, Prejudice and Pedagogy: One Director's Personal Story', in Merttens, R. and Vass, J. (Eds.), *Partnerships in Maths: Parents and Schools: The IMPACT Project*. London: Falmer Press.

Merttens, R. (1996) 'The IMPACT Project: Parental Involvement in the Curriculum, *School Effectiveness and School Improvement*, 7(4), 411–426.

Merttens, R., Mayers, D., Brown, A. and Vass, J. (Eds.) (1993) *Ruling the Margins: Problematising Parental Involvement*. London: University of North London.

Merttens, R. and Newland, A. (1996) 'Home Works: Shared Maths and Shared Writing', in Bastiani, J. and Wolfendale, S. (Eds.), *Home-School Work in Britain, Review, Reflection and Development*. London: David Fulton.

Merttens, R., Newland, A. and Webb, S. (1996) *Learning in Tandem: Involving Parents in their Children's Education*. Leamington Spa: Scholastic.

Merttens, R. and Stockton, E. (1994) *The Impact Project in Haringey 1993/4: Raising Standards in Inner City Schools* (Report to the Department for Education) (GEST 19). London: University of North London.

Merttens, R. and Vass, J. (Eds.). (1993) *Partnerships in Maths: Parents and Schools: The IMPACT Project*. London: Falmer Press.

Millard, E. (1997) *New Technologies, Old Inequalities –*

Variations Found in the Use of computers by Pupils at Home with Implications for the School Curriculum. Sheffield: The Division of Education, University of Sheffield.

Miller, A. (1997) *Business and Community Mentoring in Schools* (43). Warwick: University of Warwick and DfEE.

Miller, A. (1998a) *Business and Community Mentoring in Schools* (43). London: DfEE.

Miller, A. (1998b) *The Future of Work in London: Implications for Schools (Research Briefing 01).* London: Focus Central London.

Mills, C. and Pack, C. (1992) *Small Rural Primary Schools: a Role for Parish Councils.* Cheltenham: Countryside Community Research Unit/ Cheltenham and Gloucester College of Higher Education.

Mitchell, G. (1989) 'Community Education and School: A Commentary', in Allen, G. and Martin, I. (Eds.), *Community Education: An Agenda for Educational Reform.* Milton Keynes: Open University Press.

Monck, L. and Husbands, C. (1996) 'Education 2000: Collaboration and Cooperation as a Model of Change Management', in Bridges, D. and Husbands, C. (Eds.), *Consorting and Collaborating in the Education Marketplace.* London: Falmer Press.

Moore, C. (1994) *Partners or Pests? Experiences of Grievance and Redress Procedures in Education* (60). Edinburgh: Scottish Council for Research in Education.

Morgan, A. (1996) 'Managing the Changing Power Bases – Parents, Schools and Governors', in Bastiani, J. and Wolfendale, S. (Eds.), *Home-School Work in Britain, Review, Reflection and Development.* London: David Fulton.

Morgan, A. (1997) *Roald Dahl Family Literacy Initiative.* London: Education Extra.

Morgan, A. (1999) *Family Learning Audit. A Summary of Existing Practice.* Kingston upon Hull: Kingston upon Hull Education Action Zone.

Morgan, A. and Piccos, J. (1997) 'Working with Parents to Manage Children's Behaviour', in Tattum, D. and Herbert, G. (Eds.), *Bullying, Home, School and Community.* London: David Fulton.

Morgan, A. and Tremere, P. (1993) 'IMPACT: A Humberside Perspective', in Merttens, R. and Vass, J. (Eds.), *Partnerships in Maths: Parents and Schools: The IMPACT Project.* London: Falmer Press.

Morgan, V., Fraser, G., Dunn, S. and Cairns, E. (1993) 'A New Order of Cooperation and Involvement? Relationships between Parents and Teachers in the Integrated Schools', *Educational Review*, 45(1), 43–52.

Mortimore, P., Sammons, P., Stoll, L., Lewis, P. and Erob, R. (1988) *School Matters: The Junior Years.* Wells: Open Books.

Morton, S. (1996a) *Family Learning in West Glamorgan.* Swansea: Community and Outdoor/ Residential Education and YMCA.

Morton, S. (1996b) *Review and Evaluation of Courses*

Offered by Swansea Community Outdoor Residential Education Service. Swansea: City and County of Swansea.

Morton, S. (1998a) 'Family Learning and its Role in School Improvement. *School Enquiry and Research Newsletter (3)* City and County of Swansea.

Morton, S. (1998b) *A Survey of Recent Research, Rationale and Current Thinking about Family Learning.* Swansea: City and County of Swansea.

Morton, S. and Thomas, J.M. (1995) 'Parents and Children Working Together'. *Family Literacy News* (6), 5–6.

Moses, D. and Croll, P. (1996) 'Specialist Pastoral Care in the Primary School: A Case Study'. *Pastoral Care in Education*, 14(2), 33–38.

Munn, P. (Ed.) (1993) *Parents and Schools. Customers, Managers or Partners?* London and New York: Routledge.

Munn, P. (1994) 'The Early Development of Literacy and Numeracy Skills', *European Early Childhood Education Research Journal*, 2(1), 5–17.

Munn, P. (1998) 'Parental Influence on School Policy: Some Evidence from Research', *Journal of Education Policy*, 13(3), 379–394.

Munn, P., Cullen, M.A., Johnstone, M. and Lloyd, G. (1996) *Exclusions and In-school Alternatives.* Edinburgh: Moray House Institute of Education.

Munn, P. and Holroyd, C. (1989) *Pilot School Boards: Experiences and Achievements.* Edinburgh: Scottish Council for Research in Education.

Munro, C. (1993) 'Parental Involvement in Strathclyde Initiatives', in Merttens, R. *et al.* (Eds.), *Ruling the Margins: Problematising Parental Involvement.* London: University of North London.

Murphy, J. (1989) 'Does Inequality Matter Educationally', in Macleod, F. (Ed.), *Parents and Schools: The Contemporary Challenge.* London: Falmer Press.

National Commission On Education (1996) *Success Against the Odds: Effective Schools in Disadvantaged Areas.* London: Routledge.

National EBP Network (1998) *Developing 2020 Vision* (leaflet). Ferryhill: National EBP Network.

Newcastle City Council (1990) *Newcastle Primary Schools Enquiry Report.* Newcastle upon Tyne: Newcastle City Council.

Newton, W. (1998) 'Working in Harmony with the Community'. *School Enquiry and Research Newsletter (3)* City and County of Swansea.

North Yorkshire County Council (1998) *Report to North Yorkshire Education and Literacy Services Committee on Family Literacy Project.* North Yorkshire County Council.

O'Hagan, B. (1991) 'Fallacy: Knowledge is Power', in O'Hagan, B. (Ed.), *The Charnwood Papers: Fallacies in Community Education.* Derby: Education Now.

Owen, D. (1993) 'IMPACT at the Core of the Curriculum: the work of a Primary Maths Advisor in the New Era', in Merttens, R. and Vass, J. (Eds.), *Partnerships in Maths: Parents and Schools: The IMPACT Project*. London: Falmer Press.

Phillips, R. (1989) 'The Newham Parents' Centre: A Study of Parent Involvement as a Community Action Contribution to Inner City Community Development', in Wolfendale, S. (Ed.), *Parental Involvement: Developing Networks between School, Home and Community*. London: Cassell.

Phillips, R. (1996) 'An Urban Parent Strategy for Assessing Achievement in Literacy: Experience in The London Borough of Newham', in Wolfendale, S. and Topping, K. (Eds.), *Family Involvement in Literacy*. London: Cassell.

Poulson, L., Macleod, F., Bennett, N. and Wray, D. (1997) *Family Literacy: Practice in Local Programmes*. London: Basic Skills Agency.

Poulson, L., Bennett, N and Macleod, F. (1996) 'Researching Parental Involvement in Literacy: Current Limitations and Future Directions', *Perspectives* (54), 80–101.

Power, A. and Tunstall, R (1995) *Swimming Against The Tide*. York: Joseph Rowntree Foundation.

Powney, J., Glissov, P. and Hall, S. (1995) *The Use of Theatre Tours in Road Safety Education, Drinking, Driving and Young People* (66). Edinburgh: Scottish Council for Research in Education.

Prince's Trust (1997) *A Breakthrough to Success. Study Support, A Review*. London: The Prince's Trust.

Prince's Trust (1998) *Community Partnerships: Involving Volunteers in Study Support*. London: The Prince's Trust.

Pugh, G. (1989) 'Parents and Professionals in Pre-school Services: Is Partnership Possible?' in Wolfendale, S. (Ed.), *Parental Involvement: Developing Networks between School, Home and Community*. London: Cassell.

QPID (1997) *A Stocktake of Education Business Link Mechanisms*. London: DfEE.

QPID (1998) *TECs/CCTEs and Schools Working in Partnership*. London: DfEE.

Read On Write Away (1998) *Read On Write Away Annual Report*. Derby: Read On Write Away.

Reay, D. (1996) 'Conceptualising Choice: Social Power and Parental Involvement', *British Educational Research Journal*, 22(5), 581–596.

Reay, D. and Ball, S.J. (1997) 'Spoilt for Choice: The Working Classes and Education Markets', *Oxford Review of Education*, (28), 89–101.

Reay, D. and Ball, S.J. (1998) 'Making their Minds up: Family Dynamics of School Choice', *British Educational Research Journal*, 24(4), 431–448.

Reeves, F. (1993). *Community Need and Further Education*. Ticknall: Education Now.

Refson, B. *The Place To Be* (Information Pack). London: The Place To Be.

Reid, J., Miller, S., Tait, L., Donaldson, M., Dean, E., Thomson, G. and Grieve, R. (1996) *Pupils with*

Special Educational Needs: The Role of Speech and Language Therapists. Edinburgh: The Scottish Council For Research in Education.

Ribbens, P. (1989) 'Managing Secondary Schools after the Act: Participation and Partnership?' in Lowe, R. (Ed.), *The Changing Secondary School.* London: Falmer Press.

Richards, K. (1989) 'Neighbourhood Centres, Not Community Schools', in Allen, G. and Martin, I. (Eds.), *Community Education: An Agenda for Educational Reform.* Milton Keynes: Open University Press.

Richardson, W. (1999) 'The Workplace as a Site for Learning', in Forrest, G. (Ed.), *Work Experience for the 21st Century.* Centre for Education and Industry.

Riddell, S., Brown, S. and Duffield, J. (1994) 'Parental Power and Special Educational Needs: the Case of Specific Learning Difficulties, *British Educational Research Journal,* 20(3), 327–344.

Rushton, A. (1995) 'Get Them Young: The Impact of Early Intervention on Social and Emotional Development', in Farrell, P. (Ed.), *Children with Emotional and Behavioural Difficulties, Strategies for Assessment and Intervention.* London: Falmer Press.

Rutter, M., Maughan, B., Mortimore, P. and Ouston, J. (1979) *Fifteen Thousand Hours: Secondary Schools and their Effects on Children.* London: Open Books.

Sainsbury, M., Caspall, L., McDonald, A. and Ravenscroft, L. (1995) *Evaluation of Summer Literacy Schools.* London: National Foundation for Educational Research.

Sallis, J. (1988) *Schools, Parents and Governors. A New Approach to Accountability.* London: Routledge.

Sammons, P., Hillman, J. and Mortimore, P. (1997) 'Key Characteristics of Effective Schools: A Review of School Effectiveness Research', in White, J. and Barber, M. (Eds.), *Perspectives on School Effectiveness and School Improvement.* London: Institute of Education, University of London.

Samson, A. and Hart, G. (1995) 'A Whole School Approach to the Management of Pupil Behaviour', in P. Farrell (Ed.), *Children with Emotional and Behavioural Difficulties, Strategies for Assessment and Intervention.* London: Falmer Press.

Sandler, A. (1989) 'PACE: Parental Involvement in a Learning Through Reading Programme', in Wolfendale, S. (Ed.), *Parental Involvement: Developing Networks between School, Home and Community.* London: Cassell.

Sandow, S., Stafford, D. and Penny, S. (1987) *An Agreed Understanding? Parent-Professional Communication and the 1981 Act.* Windsor: NFER-Nelson.

Saunders, L. and Morris, M. (1995). *The National Evaluation of Urban Compacts 1991–1994.* London: NFER.

Save the Children (1996) *Ticket to Learn – Securing Children's Rights to Education. A Report of the Pilot Year.* Newcastle upon Tyne: Save the Children, Family Support Development Unit.

Sayer, J. (1989) 'Facing Issues in Parents' Responsibility for Education', in Wolfendale, S.

(Ed.), *Parental Involvement: Developing Networks between School, Home and Community.* London: Cassell.

Schagen, S. (1997) *The Evaluation of NatWest Face 2 Face with Finance.* London: NFER.

Schellekens, P. (1998) *Family Numeracy Project: Counting with Confidence.* London: North West London TEC.

Scottish Office (1998a) *Communities: Change Through Learning. Report of a Working Group on the Future of Community Education.* Edinburgh: Scottish Office.

Scottish Office (1998b) *The Excellence Fund for Schools* (Circular No. 4/98). Edinburgh: Scottish Office.

Scottish Office (1998c) *New Community Schools.* Edinburgh: Scottish Office.

Scottish Office (1998d) *Parents as Partners: Enhancing the Role of Parents in School Education. A Discussion Paper.* Edinburgh: Scottish Office.

Scottish Office (1999a) *New Community Schools: Development Seminars, Report of the Proceedings.* Edinburgh: Scottish Office.

Scottish Office (1999b) *Targeting Excellence. Modernising Scotland's Schools* (4247). Edinburgh: Scottish Office.

Sebba, J. and Sachdev, D. (1997) *What Works in Inclusive Education.* Ilford: Barnardos.

Sharland, P. (1996) 'Parenting Education in Secondary Schools – The Greater Manchester Project', in Utting, D. (Ed.), *Families and Parenting.* London: Family Policy Studies Centre.

Shaw, J. (1991). *An Investigation of Parents' Conceptual Development in the Context of Dialogue with a Community Teacher.* PhD, University of Newcastle.

Sheffield (1998) *Joint Agency Approach to Family Support, Second Draft 1998.* Sheffield: Community Health Sheffield, Sheffield City Council (Education, Leisure, Housing, Social Services) Sheffield Health, Sheffield Voluntary Sector.

Sheffield Education Dept. (1998) 'The Role of SUMES in Multi-Level Working in Sheffield', in DIECEC (Ed.), *Pathways to Intercultural Education and Raising Achievement.* Bradford: DIECEC.

Sheffield LEA (1998) *Strategies for Helping Families with Behaviour Problem Children, The C'mon Everybody Programme.* Sheffield: Sheffield LEA.

Shiner, M. and Newburn, T. (1996) *Young People, Drugs and Peer Education: An Evaluation of the Youth Awareness Programme, Home Office Drugs Prevention Initiative Paper 13.* London: HMSO.

Shucksmith, J. and Wood, S. (1998) *Keep a Cool Head – Drug Education in Primary Schools.* Edinburgh: Scottish Council for Research in Education.

Siraj-Blatchford, I. and Brooker, L. (1998) *Parent Involvement in Primary Schools in One LEA: Final Report.* London: Institute of Education, University of London.

Smith, G. (1997) 'The Safer Schools-Safer Cities Bullying Project', in Tattum, D. and Herbert, G.

(Eds.), *Bullying, Home, School and Community*. Lincoln: David Fulton.

Smith, T. (1988) 'Parents and Pre-school', in Bastiani, J. (Ed.), *Parents and Teachers 2, From Policy to Practice*. London: NFER-Nelson.

Social Exclusion Unit (1998) *Bringing Britain Together Again: A National Strategy for Neighbourhood Renewal* (Cm. 4045). London: The Stationery Office.

Stacy, M. (1991) *Parents and Teachers Together*. Milton Keynes: Open University Press.

Stern, J. (1997) *Homework and Study Support: A Guide to Teachers and Parents*. London: David Fulton.

Stoker, D. (1996) '"It hurts my heart when my child brings home a book" Reading at Home for Bilingual Families', in Bastiani, J. and Wolfendale, S. (Eds.), *Home-School Work in Britain, Review, Reflection and Development*. London: David Fulton.

Stoll, L. (1996) 'The Role of Partnerships and Networking in School Improvement', in Barber, M. and Dann, R. (Eds.), *Practical Initiatives in Action*. London: Cassell.

Strahan, H. (1994) 'You feel like you belong: Establishing Partnerships between Parents and Educators', in Abbott, L. and Rodger, R. (Eds.), *Quality in the Early Years*. Buckingham and Philadelphia: Open University Press.

Strathclyde, University of (1996) *Schools Speak for Themselves: Towards a Framework for Self-Evaluation. Report on Research for NUT*. Strathclyde: University of Strathclyde for NUT.

Street, P. and Rennie, J. (1996) *Business as Co-Educators*. Coventry: Community Education Development Centre.

Suffolk County Council (1997) *Old Warren House Parent Partnership Project: Report and Evaluation*. Ipswich: Suffolk County Council, Education.

Suffolk LEA (1998a) *Report to Suffolk LEA on a Parent Consultation Exercise For Behaviour Support Plan*. Ipswich: Suffolk LEA.

Suffolk LEA (1998b) *A Summary Report of Issues Considered During a Workshop For Parents in School*. Suffolk LEA.

Sullivan, M. (1995) 'The Perspective from an Urban Primary School', in Macbeth, A. *et al.* (Eds.), *Collaborate or Compete? Educational Partnerships in a Market Economy*. London: Falmer Press.

Sutton, A. (1998) *Conductive Education as Exemplar of the Emerging Paradigm of Dynamic Inclusion, with New Emphasis For Educational Research*. Paper presented at the European Conference on Educational Research, Ljubljana.

Swansea City and County of (1996) *Parents and Children Working Together, Family Learning Team Annual Review and Report*. Swansea: City and County of Swansea.

Swansea City and County of (1997) *Parents and Children Working Together, Family Learning Team Annual Review and Report*. Swansea: City and County of Swansea.

Swansea City and County of (1998) *Parents and*

Children Working Together, Annual Review and Report. Swansea: City and County of Swansea.

Taylor, L. and Smith, J. (1993) 'Practising Mathematics Education: A Context for IMPACT', in Merttens, R. and Vass, J. (Eds.), *Partnerships in Maths: Parents and Schools: The IMPACT Project.* London: Falmer Press.

Taylor, R. (1991) *Artists in Wigan Schools.* London: Calouste Gulbenkian Foundation.

Templeton, J. (1989) 'Creation of a Home Council in a Secondary School', in Wolfendale, S. (Ed.), *Parental Involvement: Developing Networks between School, Home and Community.* London: Cassell.

Tett, L. and Crowther, J. (1998) 'Families at a Disadvantage: Class, Culture and Literacies', *British Educational Research Journal,* 24(4), 449–460.

Thameside Infant and Junior School (1996) *Thameside Home/School Link Project.* Grays: Thameside Infant and Junior School.

Thameside Infant and Junior School (1997) *Thameside Home/School Link Project.* Grays: Thameside Infant and Junior School.

Thody, A. (1995) 'The Governor Citizen: Agent of the State, the Community or the School?' in Macbeth, A. *et al.* (Eds.), *Collaborate or Compete? Educational Partnerships in a Market Economy.* London: Falmer Press.

Thomas, G. (1992) *Effective Classroom Teamwork: Support or Intrusion.* London: Routledge.

Thomas, G. (1993) 'Special Needs, Parents and the Education Reform Act', in Merttens, R. and Vass, J. (Eds.), *Partnerships in Maths: Parents and Schools: The IMPACT Project.* London: Falmer Press.

Thomas, H. (1989) 'Who Will Control the Secondary School in the 1990s', in Lowe, R. (Ed.), *The Changing Secondary School.* London: Falmer Press.

Thomson, A.K. (1996). *Discovery and Learning. An Investigation into the Development of Social and Environmental Awareness in a Primary School.* Edinburgh: Scottish Council for Research in Education.

Tizard, J., Schofield, W.N. and Hewison, J. (1982) 'Collaboration Between Teachers and Parents in assisting Children's Reading', *British Journal of Educational Psychology* (52), 1–15.

Todd, E.S. and Higgins, S. (1998) 'Powerlessness in Professional and Parent Partnerships', *British Journal of Sociology of Education,* 19(2), 227–236.

Tomlinson, J. (1991) 'Community Education: An Assessment and the Challenge for the Future', *British Journal of Educational Studies,* 39(1), 59–64.

Tomlinson, S. (1993) 'Ethnic Minorities, Involved Partners or Problem Parents?' in Munn, P. (Ed.), *Parents and Schools. Customers, Managers or Partners.* London and New York: Routledge.

Tomlinson, S. and Vincent, C. (1997) 'Home-School Relationships: The Swarming of Disciplinary Mechanisms', *British Educational Research Journal,* 23(3), 361–377.

Toomey, D. (1989) 'Linking Class and Gender Inequality: the Family and Schooling', *British Journal of Sociology of Education*, 10(4), 389–402.

Toomey, D. (1993) 'Can Parental Involvement in Schools Increase Educational Inequality', in Merttens, R. *et al.* (Eds.), *Ruling the Margins: Problematising Parental Involvement*. London: University of North London.

Topping, K. (1991) 'Achieving More with Less: Raising Standards via Parental Involvement and Peer Tutoring', *Support for Learning*, 6(3), 112–115.

Topping, K. (1995) *Paired Reading Spelling and Writing. The Handbook for Teachers and Parents.* London: Cassell.

Topping, K. (1996a) 'The Effectiveness of Family Literacy', in Wolfendale, S. and Topping, K. (Eds.), *Family Involvement in Literacy.* London: Cassell.

Topping, K. (1996b) 'Tutoring Systems for Family Literacy', in Wolfendale, S. and Topping, K. (Eds.), *Family Involvement in Literacy.* London: Cassell.

Topping, K. and Bamford, J. (1988) *Parental Involvement and Peer Tutoring in Mathematics and Science. Developing Paired Maths into Paired Science.* London: David Fulton.

Topping, K. and Whitely, M. (1990) 'Participant Evaluation of Parent-tutored projects in reading', *Educational Research*, 32(1), 14–27.

Topping, K. and Wolfendale, S. (1995) 'The Effectiveness of Family Literacy Programmes', *Reading*, 29(3) 26–33.

Turner, E., Lloyd, J., Stronach, I. and Waterhouse, S. (1994) *Plotting Partnership: Education Business Links in Scotland. Report for the Scottish Office Education Department. Appendices and References.* Stirling: Department of Education, University of Stirling.

Tye, C. (1993) 'IMPACT and The Early Years Classroom', in Merttens, R. and Vass, J. (Eds.), *Partnerships in Maths: Parents and Schools: The IMPACT Project.* London: Falmer Press.

Utting, D. (1996) *Reducing Criminality Among Young People: A Sample of Relevant Programmes in the United Kingdom.* London: Home Office.

Vernon, J. and Sinclair, R. (1998) *Maintaining Children in Schools: The Contribution of Social Service Departments.* London: National Children's Bureau.

Vincent, C. (1993) 'Education for the Community. *British Journal of Educational Studies*, 41(4), 366–380.

Vincent, C. (1995) 'School, Community and Ethnic Minority Parents', in Tomlinson, S. and Craft, M. (Eds.), *Ethnic Relations and Schooling: Policy and Practice in the 1990s.* London: Athlone.

Vincent, C. (1996a). 'Parent Empowerment? Collective Action and Inaction', *Oxford Review of Education*, 22(4), 465–482.

Vincent, C. (1996b) *Parents and Teachers, Power and Participation.* London: Falmer Press.

Vincent, C. (1997) 'Community and Collectivism: the role of Parent Organisations in the Education System', *British Journal of Sociology of Education*, 18(2), 271–283.

Vincent, C. and Tomlinson, S. (1998) 'The Perils of Partnership', *Topic*, 20(12).

Vincent, C. and Warren, S. (1997) 'A Different Kind of Professionalism. Case Studies of the Work of Parent Organisations, *International Journal of Inclusive Education*, 1(2), 143–161.

Vincent, C. and Warren, S. (1998a) 'Becoming a Better Parent? Motherhood, Education and Transition', *British Journal of Sociology of Education*, 19(2), 177–193.

Vincent, C. and Warren, S. (1998b) *Supporting Refugee Children: A Focus on Home School Links*. Warwick: Institute of Education, University of Warwick.

Vincent, C. and Warren, S. (1999) 'Class, Race and Collective Action', in Riddell, S. and Salisbury, J. (Eds.), *Gender Equality Policies and Educational Reforms in the United Kingdom*. London: Routledge, forthcoming.

Walker, B.M. (1998a) 'Meetings Without Communication: A Study of Parents' Evenings in Secondary Schools', *British Educational Research Journal*, 24(4), 163–178.

Walker, B.M. (1998b) *Parents' Evenings at the Secondary School*. Centre for Applied Research in Education, University of East Anglia.

Waller, H. and Waller, J. (1998) *Linking Home and School, Partnerships in Practice in Primary Education*. London: David Fulton.

Warwick, D. (1995) 'Schools and Businesses', in Macbeth, A. *et al.* (Eds.), *Collaborate or Compete? Educational Partnerships in a Market Economy*. London: Falmer Press.

Watt, J.S. (1989) 'Community Education and Parental Involvement: a Partnership in Need of a Theory', in Macleod, F. (Ed.), *Parents and Schools: The Contemporary Challenge*. London: Falmer Press.

Webb, R. and Vulliamy, G. (1996) 'Headteachers as Social Workers: The Hidden Side of Parental Involvement in Primary School', *Education 3–13*, 23–31.

Wei, L. (1993) *Mother Tongue Maintenance in a Chinese Community School in Newcastle upon Tyne: Developing a Social Network Perspective*. Newcastle upon Tyne: Dept. of Speech, University of Newcastle.

Welsh, T. (1997a) 'Bullying, Home, School and Community', in Tattum, D. and Herbert, G. (Eds.), *Bullying, Home, School and Community*. London: David Fulton.

Welsh, T. (1997b) 'Seeking to Develop a Whole Community Response', in Tattum, D. and Herbert, G. (Eds.), *Bullying, Home, School and Community*. London: David Fulton.

West, A., Noden, P. and Edge, A. (1998) 'Parental Involvement in Education In and Out of School', *British Educational Research Journal*, 24(4), 461–483.

Wetz, D. (1996) *Counselling in Schools Project*. NSPCC.

Whalley, M. (1997) *Working with Parents*. London: Hodder and Stoughton.

White, J. and Barber, M. (Eds.). (1997)

Perspectives on School Effectiveness and School Improvement. London: Institute of Education, University of London.

Whitty, G., Edwards, T. and Gewirtz, S. (1993) *Specialisation and Choice in Urban Education: The City Technology College Experiment.* London: Routledge.

Whyte, B. (1997) 'Crossing Boundaries: An Exercise in Partnership Provision', *British Journal of Social Work,* 27, 679–704.

Williams, M. (1993) 'IMPACT Changes in a Support Teacher's Role', in Merttens, R. and Vass, J. (Eds.), *Partnerships in Maths: Parents and Schools: The IMPACT Project.* London: Falmer Press.

Williamson, B., Cummings, B., Bryans, P. and Newsom, C. (1998) *Absent from School: A Report of Research, Higher Horizons Project.* Durham: Department of Continuing Education, University of Durham.

Willis, P. (1990) *Moving Culture: An Enquiry into the Cultural Activities of Young People.* London: Calouste Gulbenkian Foundation.

Wilson, V., Pirrie, A. and McFall, E. (1996) *Progress in Partnership, Evaluations of Education Business Links and Teacher Placement* (73). Edinburgh: Scottish Council for Research in Education.

Wolfendale, S. (1988) *The Parental Contribution To Assessment.* The National Council for Special Education.

Wolfendale, S. (1989) 'Parental Involvement and Power-sharing in Special Needs', in Wolfendale, S. (Ed.), *Parental Involvement: Developing Networks*

between School, Home and Community. London: Cassell.

Wolfendale, S. (1992) *Empowering Parents and Teachers Working for Children.* London: Cassell.

Wolfendale, S. (1993) 'Parent's Contribution to Assessing, Recording and Communicating their Children's Development and Progress: Review and Prospects', in Merttens,R. *et al.* (Eds.), *Ruling the Margins: Problematising Parental Involvement.* London: University of North London.

Wolfendale, S. (1995) 'Involving Parents in Assessment: A Review of Approaches Facilitating Home-School Partnerships in Recording Progress', *Topic,* 14(1).

Wolfendale, S. (1996a) 'The Contribution of Parents to Children's Achievement in School: Policy and Practice in the London Borough of Newham', in Bastiani, J. and Wolfendale, S. (Eds.), *Home-School Work in Britain, Review, Reflection and Development.* London: David Fulton.

Wolfendale, S. (1996b) 'The Relationship between Parental Involvement and Educational Achievement in Parents', in Cullingford, C. (Ed.), *Parents, Education and the State.* London: Arena.

Wolfendale, S. (1996c) 'Transitions and Continuities in Home-School Reading and Literacy', in Wolfendale, S. and Topping, K. (Eds.), *Family Involvement in Literacy.* London: Cassell.

Wolfendale, S. (1997a) *Partnership with Parents in Action.* Tamworth: NASEN.

Wolfendale, S. (1997b) *Working With Parents after the*

Code of Practice. London: David Fulton.

Wolfendale, S. (1998) *City Challenge: Action for Achievement, Fifth and Final Evaluation Report.* London: London Borough of Newham.

Wolfendale, S. and Cook, G. (1997) *Evaluation of SEN Parent Partnership Schemes.* London: DfEE.

Woods, P. (1996) 'Choice, Class and Effectiveness', *School Effectiveness and School Improvement*, 7(4), 324–341.

Wymer, K. (1996) *Further Education and Democracy: The Community College Alternative.* Bilston College Publications and Education Now.

Wyndcliffe Junior School Birmingham (1998) 'Multi-Level Working in Schools', in DIECEC (Ed.), *Pathways to Intercultural Education and Raising Achievement.* Bradford: DIECEC.

Wyness, M.G. (1996) *Schooling, Welfare and Parental Responsibility.* London: Falmer Press.

Appendix: Search methodology

A number of methods were employed to identify and access relevant literature. These included standard bibliographic searches, web searches and letter writing. Indeed, we anticipated that much of the evidence would be contained in unpublished internal reports and documents generated by TECs, LEAs, charitable bodies and other organisations. Consequently, a significant proportion of the literature we accessed was recommended or identified to us by relevant organisations and individuals. Throughout the search the following keywords and search terms were used:

Home School
Parental involvement
Education/School partnerships
Family School
Parental participation
Education/Education partnerships
Parent School
Community involvement
Education/School business
Community School
Community participation
Education/School industry
Education/School Collaboration

These were adapted and added to depending on which information source was being searched; for instance using the terms school or learning in education databases generates thousands of references but not in databases such as the Home Office website.

Standard bibliographic literature search
- Library Catalogues and indexes including ERIC, BIDS and First Search

Web search
- Basic Skills Agency

www.basic-skills.co.uk
- Community Education Development Centre
  www.cedc.org.uk/contact/index.htm
- CRU- Scottish Office
  www.scotland.gov.uk/cru/default.htm
- DfEE
  http://www.open.gov.uk/dfee/dfeehome.htm
- Education Line
  www.leeds.ac.uk/educol/BEID.html
- Home Office
  http://www.homeoffice.gov.uk/
- Informal Education
  www.infed.org
- National Children's Bureau
  www.ncb.org.uk/research.htm
- National Foundation for Educational Research
  www.NFER.ac.uk/index.htm
- Scottish Council for Research in Education
  www5.ucs.edinburgh.ac.uk
- Stationery Office
  www.the-stationery-office.co.uk

References were also identified from bibliographies in the literature itself. As such, citations have been followed in a snowballing search method.

Letters were sent to all Local Education Authorities and all TECs. They were also sent to a number of children's and educational charities, educational organisations, government bodies and professional organisations. These are listed below:

Organisation Name
Advisory Centre for Education, London
Analytical Services, DfEE, London
Barnardos, Ilford
Basic Skills Agency, London
Basingstoke Consortium, Basingstoke
Bexley EBP, Welling
Bromley EBP, Bromley

Cadbury Trust, Birmingham

Calouste Gulbenkian Foundation, London

Catholic Education Service For England and Wales, London

CEDC, Coventry

Children in Scotland, Edinburgh

CNPR Division, Ofsted, London

Community Matters – National Federation Of Community Organisations, London

Croydon EBP, Croydon

Department Of Education Studies, University Of York, York

Department Of Psychology, University Of East London, London

Dept of Psychology, University Of Dundee, Dundee

DIECEC, Bradford

Eastleigh Action For Skills – Enterprise And Learning Ltd. Eastleigh

Family Links, Oxford

FCT, Newry

First Partnership Ltd, Education Business Partnership Centre, Basingstoke

Further Education Development Agency, London

General Synod Board Of Education, London

Greenwich EBP, London

Health Education Authority, London

Herefordshire EAZ, Hereford

Include, Cambridge

Institute Of Education, Warwick University, Coventry

Kids' Club Network, London

Lewisham EBP, London

London Institute Of Education, London

Moray House Institute of Education, Edinburgh University, Edinburgh

NACRO – The Services Dept. London

NAPCE, Coventry

NASEN, Coventry

NASUWT, Birmingham

National Children's Bureau, London

National Association of Governors and Managers, Birmingham

National Council for Voluntary Youth Services, London

National Council of Voluntary Childcare Organisations, London

National Foundation for Educational Research in England and Wales, Slough

National Governors' Council, Crediton

National Literacy Trust, London

National Pyramid Trust, London

NCH Action for Children, London

NSPCC, Bristol

NUT, London

Parent Network, London

Parenting Forum, London

Portsmouth and SE Hampshire EBP Ltd, Portsmouth

Prince's Trust, London

Read On, Write Away, Matlock

Save the Children (UK), London

School Of Education, Oxford Brookes University, Oxford

School Of Education, University Of Leeds, Leeds

School Of Health, De Montfort University, Leicester

Schools Provision and Organisation Division, The Scottish Office, Edinburgh

Scottish Council for Research in Education, Edinburgh

Skills Enterprise and Training Partnership Ltd., Andover

Social Exclusion Unit, Cabinet Office, London

Social Sciences Research Centre, South Bank University, London

Southampton and Forest Headstart Ltd., Southampton

Standards and Effectiveness Unit, DfEE, Westminster

Sutton EBP, Carsholton

Thames Valley Partnership, Chinnor

The National Youth Agency, Leicester

The Place to Be, London

Trust For the Study of Adolescence, Brighton

YMCA, London.

Youth Access, London

Youth Action; Crime Concern, Swindon